AF697272

SELF-DIRECTED IRAs FOR THE ACTIVE INVESTOR

SELF-DIRECTED IRAs FOR THE ACTIVE INVESTOR

Revised Edition

PETER D. HEERWAGEN

PROBUS PUBLISHING COMPANY
Chicago, Illinois

© PETER D. HEERWAGEN, 1987

ALL RIGHTS RESERVED. No part of this publication may be reproduced, stored in a retrieval system, or transmitted, in any form or by any means, electronic, mechanical, photocopying, recording, or otherwise, without the prior written permission of the publisher and the copyright holder.

This publication is designed to provide accurate and authoritative information in regard to the subject matter covered. It is sold with the understanding that the publisher is not engaged in rendering legal, accounting or other professional service. If legal advice or other expert assistance is required, the services of a competent professional person should be sought.

FROM A DECLARATION OF PRINCIPLES JOINTLY ADOPTED BY A COMMITTEE OF THE AMERICAN BAR ASSOCIATION AND A COMMITTEE OF PUBLISHERS.

Library of Congress Cataloging in Publication Data

Heerwagen, Peter D.
Self directed IRAs for the active investor.

Includes index.
1. Individual retirement accounts. I. Title.
HG1660.A3H44 1987 332.024'01 86-25312
ISBN 0-917253-61-2

Library of Congress Catalog Card No. 86-25312

Printed in the United States of America

1 2 3 4 5 6 7 8 9 0

Preface

It was not too long ago that the Individual Retirement Account was but a $1,500 (then, the maximum contribution) tax deduction—a yearly contribution destined for a money market account under the trusteeship of a bank or an insurance company. From the start, the tax deduction had great appeal, but very few gave much thought to the account itself—it was considered to be more of a savings account than an investment asset.

Although, technically speaking, the distinction between savings and investments easily blurs, in terms of real dollars and cents it is a distinction worth making. The magic of compounding—and particularly tax deferred compounding—beautifully illustrates this point.

If you earn 10 percent on yearly IRA contributions of $2,000, your account in twenty-five years will be worth nearly $220,000; if you earn 15 percent over the same period with the same yearly contributions, your account will be worth around $500,000. *It's amazing what 5 percent can mean!*

It's also amazing how large of a financial asset your IRA can become if you treat it as an investment. This means that IRA investments must be properly selected and your IRA portfolio must be managed in a manner that continually optimizes profit opportunities.

Self-Directed IRAs for the Active Investor will show you how to do all of this by using a flexible, self-directed account approach to building your IRA. In short (to return to my illustration), it is intended to help you achieve that "5 percent difference."

Peter D. Heerwagen

Contents

Introduction

Recent changes in the tax law make it more imperative than ever that persons owning IRAs regard them as investment funds that need to be managed actively. Although some of their tax benefits have been reduced by the Tax Reform Act of 1986, IRAs continue to be one of the best "tax shelters" around. In fact, they're now one of the few that remain.

Tax deferral, coupled with the magic of compounding earnings, makes the IRA a powerful builder of retirement nest eggs. The provision for the tax-deferred buildup of earnings on IRA portfolios remains in the tax code. It's available to anyone who contributes up to $2,000 to their IRA, whether or not they're also eligible to deduct contributions from their adjusted gross income.

For example, consider a person in the 28 percent tax bracket who tries to build a retirement fund without using an IRA. He sets aside $2,000 a year and earns 10 percent on the funds. After paying taxes on those earnings, he would accumulate $139,500 after 25 years. However, someone who put the same amount into an IRA accumulates $216,000 thanks to the tax deferral of the earnings. That person's nest egg is 55 percent larger.

The stock and bond markets made major advances in 1985 and 1986. Individuals with well diversified IRA funds in stocks, mutual funds, and long-term bonds did very well compared to those with IRA funds in bank CDs. The former group generated total returns (defined as current income plus capital appreciation) greater than 20 percent during 1985. The latter saw interest rates on their CD rollovers drop into the single digits, a far cry from the double digit rates of previous years.

Someone who diversified an IRA protfolio in 1985 by putting one third in the stock market, one third in the bond market, and one third in a money market fund, did much better than a person who was 100 percent invested in certificates of deposit. Assuming the stock and bond investments did just as well as the market averages in 1985 (up 31.6 percent for the S&P 500 and up 30.1 percent for the Salomon Brothers Long-Term Bond Index), then the active IRA investor realized an overall return of 23.2 percent, if the money market funds earned 8 percent. The inactive IRA investor, on the other hand, only realized a 10 percent return on his bank CD investment—a significant 13.2 percent less than the active investor.

The lesson should be clear. The risk of "riskless" IRA investments is in the lost opportunity of not participating in rising debt and equity markets. Although the financial markets will rarely perform as well as they did in 1985, IRA owners need to have assets positioned to take advantage of such occurrences.

Unfortunately, the American public still holds almost 70 percent of all IRA funds in what could be called no risk/low return investment vehicles (i.e., banks and insurance companies). This percentage would be even higher if money market mutual funds were segregated from the mutual fund category as a whole. Based on one management company survey, this could amount to another 5 percent, which means a total of 75 percent of all IRA funds are invested very conservatively.

Recently, a few people have begun to move their IRA investments from the ultra conservative banks, money market funds, and insurance companies into what are known as "self-directed" IRAs (see the following chart). These IRAs give their owners maximum flexibility in investing funds, thus allowing them to take advantage of higher returns than those offered by banks and insurance companies.

A few extra percentage points in yield makes a big difference over time, especially when it's compounding on a tax-deferred basis. For example, $2,000 contributed each year to an IRA that earns 8 percent will grow to $158,000 in 25 years. That same amount will increase to nearly $300,000 during the identical time period if it earns 12 percent. The 50 percent higher return generates 100 percent more assets!

	IRA Market Share		
	1983	*1984*	*1985*
Banks*	70.5%	65.6%	61.0
Mutual funds	12.4	12.2	15.8
Insurance companies	10.1	10.3	8.5
Self-directed	7.0	11.9	14.7
Total	100.0	100.0	100.0

* Includes commercial banks, savings banks, and credit unions.
Source: Investment Company Institute.

Investments that did well in 1985 and 1986 were those that benefited from low interest rates, a declining dollar, and a generally strong U.S. stock market. Long-term zero coupon bonds, for instance, rose 50 percent in value because they are quite sensitive to changes in interest rates. Even U.S. Treasury bonds, backed by the full faith and credit of the U.S. government, returned 32 percent in interest and capital appreciation. Mutual funds that invested in foreign securities posted gains in excess of 75 percent. These funds benefited from a declining dollar and strong overseas stock markets.

The recent economic climate indicates that inflation continues to be moderate thanks to the sharp drop in oil prices, a softening of commodity prices, competition from low-priced imported goods and slower growth in wage demands. Interest rates remain at low levels and the stock market has reached an all-time high. The S&P average has gone up four consecutive years and was strong in the first half of 1986. This phenomenon has occurred only once before—during the 1920s.

Although the economy continues to expand, there is uncertainty as to how much longer this will continue. The Federal Reserve can't push interest rates down too much more for fear of rekindling inflation. And there's still the uncertainty of the impact of tax reform and large government deficits. Will this mean more saving, less investment, or more spending on the part of the American people and business?

Currently, investors are inclined to put their money into financial assets rather than hard assets such as real estate, gold and silver, and oil and gas. Many are seeking the high yields of the junk bond funds and the Ginnie Mae funds. They're even looking at option income funds which earn income from selling options on portfolio holdings.

Earning double digit returns on IRAs clearly has become a more difficult task in an era of low interest rates, low inflation, and high stock prices.

Investments in real estate, medium-term fixed income funds, convertible bond mutual funds, and equity-income funds remain attractive for IRA investments. But make sure your IRAs are properly diversified in case one investment area turns downward. There's no guarantee that interest rates will stay low or that inflation will remain in limbo. Investors must maintain a flexible posture regarding changing market conditions. That's the challenge of a self-directed IRA.

This book shows you how to manage your retirement funds with a self-directed IRA. It explains how to start a self-directed IRA and where to look for the best results. It also tells you how to set goals and objectives, how to diversify your account properly, protect it against inflation, and measure its performance. It shows you how to apply many of the techniques professional pension fund managers use to maximize returns and minimize risk. This book provides you with the appropriate strategies.

In addition, the book reviews many of the investments suitable for self-directed IRAs. It discusses the pros and cons of each and the role of each in the total IRA portfolio. Appendixes A and B list the names and addresses of firms offering specific IRA investments in mutual funds and limited partnerships. (This listing should not be considered an endorsement of the investments by the publisher or author.)

In order to gain the proper perspective and provide a personal touch, the book presents several hypothetical case studies of persons who have IRAs and want to find the most appropriate investments to meet their goals, objectives and individual circumstances. These examples are based on changing life styles, investment needs and philosophies. Readers will be able to identify with one or more persons in these case studies, and learn from their experiences.

Appendix C provides an easy-to-use question and answer section that will serve as a guide to the more technical aspects of the management of your self-directed IRA. Appendix D presents a list of discount brokerage firms and characteristics of their IRAs. Finally, Appendix E tabulates IRA earnings on annual $2,000 contributions over 40 years, at varying yield rates.

CHAPTER 1

Why The Self-Directed IRA is Better

IRA investment dollars are starting to mount up. At the end of 1985, the nation's total investment in IRAs was a whopping $200 billion. Over $50 billion poured in during 1985 alone. Although recent changes in the tax code that limit the deductibility of IRA contributions for some persons will slow this growth, many Americans realize the IRA is one of the few vehicles that can be counted on to provide a secure retirement nest egg. By the end of the decade, IRA funds are expected to grow to as much as $500 billion, making them the second largest block of savings after corporate pension funds.

Individuals in the 45 to 54 age group are twice as likely to be IRA owners as those in the 25 to 34 year-old bracket. As people near retirement age, they understandably become much more sensitive to the need to save to build retirement funds for their years as senior citizens. Younger folks, on the other hand, have more basic financial needs to fulfill, such as starting a family and buying and furnishing a house. They may not have the discretionary savings available to fund an IRA. In addition, they're too far removed from retirement to feel the urge to squirrel money away for the future.

Unfortunately, the need for retirement savings to supplement Social Security and pension benefits is becoming that much greater as faith in the Social Security System wanes. Even with cosmetic surgery that was performed on it three years ago to stop the hemorrhaging, the System is still in weak condition. The situation promises to worsen as the number of workers paying into the system decreases relative to benefit recipients. This ratio is now 3.2 to 1: it's projected to decrease to 2 to 1 by the end of this century, which is only a few years away. Simply put, fewer workers will be supporting more retirees.

Other problems may face the average American at retirement. It's likely Congress will increase the age at which Social Security eligibility begins from 65 to 68. It's also a good bet there will be lower cost of living boosts going to future retirees. And there might even be a freeze on benefits. Meanwhile, inflation keeps slowly deflating the purchasing power of savings nest eggs, making them worth less at retirement time.

Some companies may compensate for reduced Social Security benefits by beefing up their pension plans, but don't count on it. Most are trying to minimize these costs and are cutting back on pensions instead of expanding them. Witness the number of companies who recently have converted from defined benefit to defined contribution plans. The latter don't promise a set pension payout. The employer contributes to the plan, but leaves the investment decision to employees, who assume all the attendant risks. In addition, with average employment at any one location of only 5.5 years, and with the increased mobility of the labor force, fewer and fewer workers will be eligible for corporate retirement benefits in amounts sufficient to sustain themselves after their careers end.

Where does all this leave the average worker? The smart ones will plan ahead and begin building their own retirement accounts to supplement funds they receive from Social Security and pensions. The easiest way to do this is through an IRA. If you save on your own, outside an IRA or other tax-qualified plan (Keogh, Simplified Employee Pension, or 401(k) salary reduction plan), you'll be using after-tax dollars and earnings on those dollars will be immediately taxable. IRAs, on the other hand, are funded with pre-tax dollars for those with incomes under $50,000 and the earnings are tax-deferred for all contributors. The IRA accounts can build up quite rapidly; $2,000 per year invested at 12% will add up to over $260,000 in 25 years. This is a nice piece of change to have at your disposal when the paychecks stop.

The IRAs most people are familiar with are offered by banks, mutual funds, insurance companies, and brokerage firms. However, as these institutions diversify in an attempt to provide a comprehensive array of financial services and gain market share, the divisions are becoming blurred. For example, banks are offering self-directed IRAs through affiliations with discount brokers. Insurance companies are selling what appear to be mutual funds in the guise of variable annuities. And brokerage firms are offering negotiable certificates of deposit to their IRA customers. Notwithstanding this cross-breeding of investments, the best-known financial products offered by each institution and their key characteristics are summarized in the chart below:

	Characteristic				
Type	*Safety*	*Liquidity*	*Potential Returns*	*Fees*	*Inv. Advice*
Banks					
Certificate of Dep.	High	Med.	Low	Low	None
Insurance Cos.					
Annuities	High	Med.	Med.	High	Some
Mutual Funds					
Money Market	High	High	Low	Low	None
Bond	Med.	High	Med.	Low	None
Stock	Low	High	High	Low	None
Brokerage Firms					
Stocks	Low	High	High	Med.	Yes
Partnerships	Med.	Low	High	High	Yes

As can be seen, investments offered by banks, insurance companies and mutual fund money market funds have higher degrees of safety and lower returns compared to either a stock mutual fund or a brokerage self-directed account. Basically, this is a trade-off between risk and reward. The higher the risk you're willing to take, the higher the reward. Conversely, the lower the risk, the lower the return you'll usually get.

Although this book is primarily about self-directed IRAs, it will be worthwhile taking a closer look at the other IRA vehicles by examining the pluses and minuses of each. This will serve to put them in proper perspective *vis á vis* the self-directed account.

Savings Institution IRAs

Many different types of savings institutions offer IRAs to depositors and other members of the public. These include commercial banks, savings and loan associations, and credit unions. You can usually chose between two types of investments the banks offer; either a fixed rate or variable rate instrument. With a fixed rate, you're guaranteed the stated rate over the life of the investment, which is usually the familiar certificate of deposit.

With the variable rate, the interest rate varies each month, quarter, or year. The rate is usually tied to a benchmark rate such as the prime rate or the rate paid on 90-day Treasury bills. Sometimes there are floors and ceilings outside of which the rates paid on your IRA cannot fall or rise. Banks offer variable rates through their money market-type accounts.

If you believe interest rates will drop, then you're better off locking in a fixed rate at today's higher yields. If you believe rates will rise, then you'll be ahead of the game by going for the variable yield instrument. You can convert to a fixed yield later.

Banks also offer zero coupon certificates of deposit, which are very similar to the popular zero coupon bonds. The CDs are purchased at a discount, and interest accrues and is paid out at maturity.

The advantages of savings institution IRAs are convenience, safety, and low cost. They are convenient because they can be set up at the institution with which you already have a banking relationship. Safety is obtained through the deposit insurance that insures the account up to $100,000. Naturally, you'll want to make certain this is backed by Federal insurance, not state insurance, to avoid being trapped in a repeat of the Ohio and Maryland savings bank industry debacles.

Savings institution IRAs are relatively inexpensive because usually no set-up or annual fees are charged; however, some banks impose a termination fee when you close your account. Because no IRA salespeople are on commissions in a bank, all your IRA money goes to work for you earning interest.

Saving institution IRAs have several disadvantages. They aren't very flexible, you're penalized for early withdrawals, and the returns are relatively low. With these types of IRAs, you can't move funds from one investment medium to another. You're stuck with chosing from only those investments offered by a bank or credit union—debt securities with varying maturities. If you want to change investments, you'll have to close your savings institution IRA and open another somewhere else.

Another negative is that if you have to make early withdrawals, you may forfeit interest accrued but not paid. If another, more promising investment comes along, you're locked into the bank CD, unless you're willing to take an early withdrawal penalty and lose interest income.

Finally, savings institution returns are not very exciting. They're lower than comparable corporate bond rates of the same maturity. And there's no way to enjoy the fruits of capital gain available from other investments—what you take out of the savings institution IRA is what you put in, plus interest earned.

Insurance Company IRAs

Not surprisingly, the insurance industry has made a move into the IRA market. These companies offer annuity contracts, whereby the IRA owner pays into the account for a period of time, and then the principal plus earnings are converted into an annuity stream of income for as long as he lives. Of course, the funds don't have to be converted to an annuity; they can simply be drawn out at any time and invested elsewhere.

As with the savings institutions, insurance companies offer both fixed and variable annuities. A fixed annuity promises a set rate of return for a specified time period. The returns from a variable annuity, on the other hand, are tied to the securities markets and will fluctuate depending on the success of the insurance company's portfolio managers. Variable annuities offer a choice of managed accounts: stocks, bonds and money market accounts, or possibly several more, depending on the particular insurance company. You may allocate a portion of your IRA funds to each account and then transfer assets among them, depending on how you feel towards different markets. In this respect, they're like a family of mutual funds.

The advantage of an insurance IRA is that fixed annuities are relatively safe investments with guaranteed rates of return for specified periods of time. The disadvantages are high administrative fees, sales charges, and termination fees, and generally low rates of return on investments. With insurance company contracts, you pay sales charges which are usually taken off the top of your IRA contribution. A large portion of these go to the insurance company salesperson who sold you the IRA investment. In addition, you may pay start-up fees, management fees, expense risk charges, mortality risk fees, adminsitrative fees and investment advisory fees. These can easily subtract from the investment performance of the insurance contract.

Termination fees can also be a problem. These usually scale downwards, depending on how long you've held the contract in your IRA. However, if interest rates drop shortly after you've made the investment, it could be expensive to terminate. Insurance companies usually compound interest on an annual rate, so you have to be careful when comparing yields with other investments. Also, although you can switch investments within the insurance company's family of fixed and variable rate vehicles, you don't have the flexibility to invest in anything but these limited offerings.

Money Market and Mutual Fund IRAs

Mutual funds offer IRAs through custodian banks which hold fund shares for the IRA investor. Many large mutual fund companies own a family of different funds, whereby the IRA holder can switch among them. Mutual funds invest in just about everything, including stocks, corporate bonds, convertible bonds, government securities, mortgage-backed securities, certificates of deposit, and bankers' acceptances. They provide a wide variety of investment choices for the small IRA holder.

As most people know, mutual funds are a pool of dollars under professional management that are invested according to the goals and objectives of the fund. They range in terms of risk from the most conservative money market funds to the very aggressive growth funds. Mutual funds are typically categorized as either growth, capital appreciation, income, balanced, or sector (industry) funds.

The mutual fund industry is divided into no-load and load funds. The load funds are usually recommended by a broker or financial planner who receives a commission from selling them to you. This is deducted from the amount of funds available for investment in your IRA. No-load funds may be recommended by a few financial planners and advisors, but usually you'll have to do your own legwork to pick a fund which meets your needs. With the no-loads, you have all of your money working for you in the IRA.

Several reference books provide historical data on no-load fund performances to help in the selection process. A few of the popular financial magazines also publish periodic figures on both load and no-load funds, as well as some financial newsletters which track fund performance on a weekly and monthly basis.

Mutual fund companies charge management fees as part of the operating expenses of the fund. They are deducted from interest and dividend income, and can range from one-half to one per cent of net assets under management, depending on the type of fund. In addition, the custodian bank charges relatively small $10 set-up and annual fees for handling IRA paperwork.

The primary advantage of mutual funds is that they provide a quick and easy way to spread out your IRA portfolio. They offer instant diversification which hopefully reduces risk. Another advantage is that they provide professional management of the investments in their portfolios, so you don't have to devote a large part of your own time monitoring IRA investments. A third advantage of mutual funds is that by pooling resources with other investors, you can cut down on transaction costs. Finally, you can chose a mutual fund which closely matches your IRA investment goals and objectives. And if these happen to change for any reason, you can switch among funds in a family of funds, usually without a sales charge.

The primary disadvantage of the mutual fund IRA approach is that you can't tailor the investments to match completely what you want to invest in. For example, it's hard to find a fund with 30% in bonds, 40% in stocks, 20% in real estate and 10% in money market funds. And if you wanted to change the percentages, then you'd have to search for another fund that matched up well with your portfolio requirements.

Of course, you can try to create a mix of mutual funds to match your objectives, but this may be a difficult task because the funds themselves are constantly modifying their portfolio emphasis as market conditions change. And without periodic calls to the management, you won't have knowledge of their current investment mix.

Another problem with mutual funds is picking the right one for your IRA. Figures developed by Lipper Analytical Services, a leading monitor of the mutual fund industry, show that for the fifteen-year period ended December 31, 1984, fewer than one-half of the almost 300 funds outperformed the S&P 500 composite stock index. And the results were not much better in 1985, a strong year for the stock and bond markets. In all fairness, however, it should also be pointed out that some mutual funds have done quite well for their investors over the years, generating compound growth rates in excess of 20% per year.

Although mutual fund IRAs are not considered in the same class as self-directed IRAs, they'll be emphasized in this book because in certain cases they provide valuable additions to self-directed accounts, particularly smaller ones. For example, a relatively conservative person with limited IRA funds looking for high yields cannot hope to get proper diversification by purchasing a few individual corporate bonds. The best alternative is to find a bond mutual fund where a small IRA investment can be made.

In another situation, the IRA investor may want to put funds in high growth stocks with good appreciation potential, but doesn't want to be bothered with following such stocks on a daily basis. And he doesn't have the technical knowledge of computer hardware, software, and peripheral equipment; semiconductors; telecommunications, and other high-tech businesses to do a good job of investment selection. He would rather turn that portion of his IRA portfolio over to experts at an aggressive growth mutual fund.

Here's an example of what customers at one of the large mutual fund companies are doing with their IRAs. A 1984 survey of the 200,000 IRA owners indicated that 57% were in equity funds, 31% in money market funds, while only 12% were in bond funds. The most popular funds were money market funds, aggressive growth, and growth and income funds, in that order. It's interesting to note the popularity of the stock funds with IRA mutual fund investors, probably because of the diversification and growth features they offer.

The Self-Directed IRA

Finally, we get to what this book is about: the self-directed IRA. As the name implies, this type of IRA allows you, the owner, to make the selection of investments for your account. Or you can employ the services of an advisor. You direct the portfolio through the IRA trustee or custodian. It's much like a brokerage account. You're able to invest in almost all of the securities your broker sells or anything that a non-brokerage firm trustee (an independent company) approves if your account is with it. Believe it or not, this covers just about everything imaginable, including savings bank certificates of deposit, insurance company annuities, and passbook savings accounts.

The obvious advantage of a self-directed IRA is the maximum investment control and flexibility you obtain for your IRA funds. You have the opportunity to evaluate the financial markets and then make your own investment decisions. You put yourself in charge of your pension assets.

Unlike mutual funds, there is no intermediary making the investment decisions. And you're not limited to switching among a fund manager's family of funds. You can invest in individual stocks and bonds, sell options on stocks in your portfolio, buy limited partnerships, mutual funds, government bonds, zero coupon bonds, convertible bonds, preferred stocks, and a host of other securities. You might even do the unthinkable and invest part of your self-directed funds in CDs similar to those that savings banks offer.

You have the luxury of tailoring your investments exactly to your individual needs. You may specialize or diversify as much as you want, depending on your own circumstances. Steady IRA fund inflows of $2,000 a year enable you to dollar cost average and restructure your portfolio without being forced to sell existing holdings.

The self-directed IRA owner can shoot for better than average total returns by investing in high-yielding securities or growth situations. He can take advantage of special situations when they come along without having to rely on someone else to do it for him. Most investments can be switched very quickly with a simple buy or sell order. For instance, insured CDs may be purchased through a self-directed IRA and sold at any time at current market rates, without the annoying six-month interest penalty the banks charge.

Unlike the big pension funds, you don't have to worry about upsetting the market price of a security with large buy or sell orders. You can move your IRA funds in and out of smaller companies without the market noticing. You may seek above-average returns by placing funds in relatively illiquid investments known as limited partnerships. The self-directed approach allows you to take advantage of these benefits to their maximum as you take charge of your IRA investments and built your retirement nest egg.

Self-directed accounts give IRA owners the same money management advantages enjoyed by pension funds. Like the big funds, with a self-directed IRA you're free to invest in just about anything, and there are no tax considerations as long as the retirement money is in the hands of the trustee. In fact, you have the flexibility the pension funds have and much more. You're not constrained by funding requirements, actuarial rates, liquidity needs, and turnover rates for a large number of people. With your self-directed IRA, you have only yourself and your spouse to worry about.

The primary disadvantage with using self-directed IRAs is that trustee or custodial administrative costs are somewhat higher than those charged by banks and mutual funds. You'll also pay commissions on the purchase and sale of each investment you make. Commissions on individual stocks average 2% at full service brokers and 1% at discount brokers on each IRA-size trade of between $2,000 and $5,000 principal amount. On the other hand, you don't have to contend with interest penalties on savings bank CDs, or management fees charged by mutual fund companies.

Another drawback is that you should probably have a medium to large IRA of at least $10,000 before making investments in individual securities. This will allow for adequate diversification to reduce portfolio risk. If both husband and wife have their own IRAs, then these can be considered jointly in judging the potential for proper diversification. Therefore, spouses with $7,500 each, or a total of $15,000 in their IRAs could consider purchasing individual securities.

But this should not preclude the possibility of establishing a small self-directed IRA if the funds are placed into relatively conservative investments such as zero coupon bonds, unleveraged real estate limited partnerships or investment trusts, fixed income mutual funds, or equity-income funds. In this case, diversification is not as important a factor because the very nature of these investments makes the portfolio less risky.

Simply put, the self-directed IRA is the best choice for almost anyone who is actively seeking the best investment opportunities and wants maximum flexibility in managing an IRA. As long as the risks taken are consistent with portfolio size and other personal factors, the self-directed IRA should soon become the universal IRA for almost everyone.

CHAPTER 2

Ten Rules for Successful IRA Investing

This book is all about investing your IRA funds the self-directed way. Ten basic rules should govern the management of your account. Following them will enable you to increase the odds of maximizing returns on your IRA investments, consistent with the level of risk you're willing to assume. Only the self-directed format allows you to implement fully all ten rules.

These rules form the major themes of this book. You'll find constant reference to them throughout the text, although no number references such as "Rule #1" or "Rule #2" are used. The IRA investing rules are presented here in a concise format for a quick overview of the major points in the book. It's suggested that they be reviewed several times so the concepts remain fresh in your memory as you continue through the book.

1. *Establish your IRA investment goals and objectives at the outset.* Match IRA investments to your overall investment philosophy, your stage in life, and your other investments. Determine the parameters of risk you're willing to take. Quantify objectives so that you have something to compare investment results with.

2. *Modify your IRA investment objectives as you mature and as your circumstances change.* You'll probably want your portfolio orientation to evolve from one emphasizing moderate growth to one with a more conservative flavor as you reach retirement age. Protection of assets will be the driving force at this latter stage in life, but

once again, other individual circumstances will influence your IRA investment approach.

3. *Maintain adequate liquidity in your IRA.* This will enable you to take full advantage of new investment opportunities as they come along, as well as provide readily available funds if you have to make emergency withdrawals or face mandatory distributions at age 70 and 1/2.

4. *Invest your IRA funds for the long term.* IRA investments should be made with a long-term perspective in mind, for you can't draw funds out of the account without penalty until you reach age 59 and 1/2. Unfortunately, most investors are too short-term oriented, always looking for the fast buck. Studies have shown you don't gain by constant trading, because transaction costs will eat up a large part of any profits.

5. *Invest your IRA funds for current yield.* Go for high yields with acceptable risks. As much as possible of the total return (defined as current yield plus capital gain or loss) should be current on the theory that a dollar today is worth more than a dollar received tomorrow, especially in the tax-deferred environment of an IRA. Capital gains are never assured, whereas current income is money in the bank. Investors who go for steady returns will usually do better than those who go for home runs. It's also a lot easier on the nerves.

6. *Diversify your IRA holdings.* Spreading your IRA funds over a range of investments will reduce risks, so that if one turns sour, its impact on the total portfolio will be minimal. You don't want to be dependent on any investment. A common mistake is to get too comfortable with one type of investment, be it real estate, zero coupon bonds, or whatever, and discount everything else.

7. *Protect your IRA assets against inflation.* Always keep an eye on changes in the consumer price index. Although the inflation rate has come down in recent years, it still erodes the purchasing power of the dollar. And this could hurt at retirement time. IRA portfolios should include investments that act as a hedge against inflation.

8. *Set up more than one IRA.* This will enable you to maximize the investment potential of your IRA dollars. It will give you greater flexibility. With several IRAs, you can invest in mutual funds and limited partnerships that may not be available when you have only

one IRA at your disposal. Weighing against this approach is the problem of paying too many administrative fees.

9. *Don't reinvest dividends and other cash distributions in the same IRA investment, unless you're already adequately diversified.* You should let the cash build up to the point that new investments can be made. This will enable you to diversify as fast as possible, especially in the early years when your IRA is likely to be relatively small.

10. *Periodically review your IRA's investment performance against the goals and objectives you've established.* Every so often you should take an accounting of how your IRAs are doing. Measure them against the standard market indices. Based on the results, adjustments can be made in the mix of portfolio investments. If performance is poor, replace your investment advisor; if you're managing the IRA yourself, find someone who can do a better job.

CHAPTER 3

Opening the Self-Directed IRA

In order to open up a self-directed account, you'll need to contact a stockbroker, financial planner, investment advisor, or if you handle your own financial affairs, perhaps a discount brokerage firm. You'll be given several documents to read and sign before you can begin making investments in your self-directed account. They include the plan adoption agreement, the trust/custodial agreement, and the disclosure statement. Each is reviewed later on in this chapter, so you'll have a chance to familiarize yourself with them.

The IRA Trust Concept

Unfortunately, you can't commingle IRA funds with other assets. As with corporate pension funds, IRAs must be segregated into separate accounts under the auspices of a trustee or custodian. Like IRAs offered by banks, insurance companies, and mutual funds, the self-directed IRA must have a trustee or custodian whose functions and duties are very similar when it comes to handling IRAs.

Technically, trustees are responsible for selecting investments according to the prudent person's rule, whereas custodians merely act as conduits for IRA funds. The former group holds legal title to property for the benefit of the grantor and has an implied duty to carry out transactions. A custodian administers the IRA account by handling paperwork and reporting requirements associated with the account holder's investment activity.

Theoretically, a trustee has fiduciary responsibility to review security purchases for your IRA. Some trustees do this, particularly with respect to limited partnership purchases, but for the most part IRA purchases are rubber-stamped as acceptable as long as they're legal. Most trustees only assume custodial responsibility for the securities in the self-directed IRA.

In the case of IRAs, the trustee or custodian handling the account is required by law to be a bank or other institution which satisfies certain standards and guidelines set forth by the Treasury Department. The IRS grants them permission to operate custodian or trustee accounts, and they must demonstrate a capability to show they'll administer the IRAs properly.

There are several reasons why you cannot be your own IRA trustee. To begin with, the funds need to be held by a financial institution in order to limit access to them by you, the account holder. Therefore, you have to contact the trustee of your IRA to make withdrawals; you can't do this on your own. The financial institution also provides a ready source of information about your IRA. It has computer facilities and information banks necessary to produce reports for you and the Internal Revenue Service. And finally, the institution has a continuity of existence—after your demise, payments to beneficiaries can be made with relative ease.

When setting up a self-directed IRA, you must enter into a written agreement with the trustee or custodian that establishes a legal relationship between you and the guardian of the IRA funds. The IRA application form is sometimes called the plan adoption agreement. In other words, by signing it you automatically adopt the trustee/custodial agreement.

The Internal Revenue Service allows organizations acting as trustees or custodians for IRAs to use one of two model agreements–Form 5305 for trustee accounts and Form 5305-A for custodial accounts. Sponsors using them automatically meet the legal requirements of the Internal Revenue Code. Many use the IRS forms as a convenience. Or they may get IRS approval for their own prototype trust agreement or custodial account. In this chapter both 5305 forms will be referred to as the trust agreement to simplify matters, because the roles of IRA trustee and custodian are so similar.

Trust Agreement

The trust agreement is pretty standard for all self-directed accounts, as it is with other types of IRAs. The text makes frequent reference to the Internal Revenue Code. Key points covered include the non-forfeitable interest you have in your IRA, the various limitations placed on contributions, the types of investments that are illegal, the requirements for making withdrawals, the need for grantor (i.e., you, the IRA owner) statements regarding the purpose of the withdrawal, and an indication that the trustee will provide information reports to the IRS. Some of these provisions are discussed in more detail below.

The trust agreement will state that yearly contributions are limited to $2,000 ($2,250 including a spousal account) for each tax year, with the exception of rollovers. In other words, you can't contribute more than the law permits. Contribution payments must be in cash, whereas rollovers may be in cash or property such as securities.

As far as investment of contributions is concerned, the grantor will direct the trustee to invest both contributions and any earnings on them. For administrative reasons, the trustee may place limits on the type of investments, such as all publicly-traded securities, covered call options, mutual funds, money market instruments and anything else that is available for acquisition in the regular course of business.

Some self-directed IRA trustees have more restrictive policies than others (i.e., IRA owners can't buy stocks, only limited partnerships sold by financial planners or only securities sold by a particular brokerage firm). Others allow just about anything that's legal, including private offerings, investment homes and condominium units.

The IRA holder can also delegate investment responsibility for his account to an authorized agent or attorney-in-fact by notifying the trustee in writing. Many trustees have separate forms on which to issue this delegation. This allows your broker or financial planner to execute all IRA buy and sell orders that you initiate though him.

The trust agreement will also state that any uninvested cash in your IRA will be placed in a money market mutual fund that the trustee uses. This should include automatic deposit and withdrawal of funds from all account activity, with daily posting of interest. It requires your initial authorization in writing, usually when the IRA plan adoption agreement is signed. Sometimes more than one account will be available, so you, the IRA grantor, have to choose which money market fund or bank the idle cash is to be placed in.

The trust agreement will indicate that life insurance contracts (term or whole life policies) are prohibited investments because IRAs are designed for retirement, not inheritance purposes. Collectibles are also not legal investments. These include works of art, rugs, antiques, metals, gems, stamps, coins, or anything else specified by the Treasury Secretary. Even though trustees are not in a position to buy these types of investments, they want to make the restrictions clear to IRA investors. The agreement will also specify that the participant cannot borrow any money from the IRA, nor pledge any part of the IRA as security for a loan.

With regard to withdrawals, the agreement will state that you must specify in writing to the trustee your intended disposition of any amount withdrawn. This is particularly true if you make the withdrawal before reaching age 59 and 1/2. The trustee needs to report this information to the IRS. You'll receive a form to fill out when you make the withdrawal request.

The trust agreement also puts you on notice that IRA distributions must begin at age 70 and 1/2. The owner may elect, in a manner agreeable to the trustee, to take distributions as lump sum, in equal payments or as an annuity. The elections will vary from trustee to trustee. If no choice is given, then mandatory distributions will be made in the form of a lump sum payment or by another method, such as 10% per year of the balance remaining in the account.

Another point to remember: if the grantor or his surviving spouse dies before distributions are completed, then the beneficiary must receive the balance within five years. If at the time of the participant's death, payments are being made over a fixed term, then they can continue in accordance with the participant's prior direction. However, some trustees will distribute proceeds in a shorter period of time.

The trust agreement may also specify that funds from another IRA may be transferred in or funds already in the account may be transferred out to another IRA. Under a divorce decree, funds may also be transferred to an IRA owned by a former spouse.

The powers, duties and obligations of the trustee will also be spelled out in the trust agreement. This includes the fact that it will have no discretion to direct any investments, but may hold securities in its own name. It cannot commingle funds with any other property holdings. The trustee will not guarantee funds from loss or depreciation. The IRA owner is solely responsible for the success or failure of any and all investment selections made. The trustee will keep accurate records and file periodic reports to the IRA owner, including an annual statement of account showing the fair market value of assets. It will also submit required reports to the IRS.

The trust agreement may state that the trustee can resign or be removed by the grantor upon written notice and upon appointment of a successor. Any fees due it can be deducted from the IRA. The agreement may be amended or terminated, as long as it doesn't deprive the grantor of any benefit he was entitled to for contributions made prior to the amendment.

The agreement may spell out the fee schedule, how and when fees will be deducted from the IRA account, when they may be revised, and the number of days notice that will be given prior to any revision. In addition, there may be a section of miscellaneous provisions, which includes a prohibition against assignment of benefits, particularly to a creditor, the order of liquidation of assets if the donor has failed to indicate how he wishes it to be done (or if there are no beneficiaries designated or living), and how the payment of unrelated business taxes, if any, will be made.

As is evident, the self-directed IRA trust agreement can be a rather lengthy document. Like other standard agreements, it spells out the respective duties and responsibilities of each party. The typical IRA agreement is not that complicated, but should be read and understood before you sign the application or plan adoption agreement. You don't want to be caught unawares if something unusual happens to your IRA nest egg further down the road to retirement.

Disclosure Statement

The IRS requires all IRA trustees and custodians to provide prospective IRA owners with a disclosure statement. The grantor has seven days to revoke his plan adoption agreement if he changes his mind. In that case, he's entitled to a full refund of the contribution plus all related fees and commissions. Some trustees will delay making investments for a week to ten days while this cooling off period is in effect. They don't want to have to sell securities to refund money during the revocation period. You may be asked to sign the adoption agreement without seeing the disclosure statement or the trust agreement. Don't. Insist on looking them over first.

The disclosure statement will contain explanations of certain items in plain language so everyone understands exactly what he's getting into. It's a repeat of much of what is in the trust or custodian agreement. The statement covers some of the basic requirements on eligibility and contributions, the tax effect of setting up an IRA, various restrictions and prohibited transactions, when and how to cancel your IRA, penalties for early withdrawal, and the fact that the IRA program has been blessed by the IRS.

The disclosure statement must also provide certain financial information, including a projection of the growth in value of the IRA, sales commissiions to be charged each year, and other fees and expenses. For self-directed accounts, the IRS lets the trustee and custodian give a disclaimer that it's impossible for them to estimate the value of IRA assets at any given future point in time, or that the growth in value is neither guaranteed nor projected. Some disclosure statements go on to say that future retirement benefits depend on too many unknown factors, such as contributions, earnings on them, the market value of the investments, and the goals of the IRA owner.

Selecting a Self-Directed Account Trustee or Custodian

Most investment professionals will be more than happy to handle your self-directed business. However, as with everything else, if your IRA is small or you don't have other large accounts with the firm, you may not get the type of attention you think you deserve. These professionals are usually employed by one of three types of financial firms that offer self-directed accounts: full service brokerage firms, who generally act as their own custodians; discount brokers (including those affiliated with banks); and financial planning firms, who often use independent trustees for their clients' IRAs.

If you don't already have an advisor, find one you can be comfortable with and who has an investment philosophy that's compatible with yours. You'll also want a counselor that occasionally comes up with some good investment ideas, who's willing to spend some time with you, and who has some expertise on the financial markets and a good track record with the kinds of investments you're interested in for your IRA. The person you select as your advisor will be much more important to your IRA success than the self-directed trustee or custodian you chose.

You can have as many individual retirement accounts as you want with as many different trustees, custodians, banks, and mutual funds. Naturally, you'll pay set up and administrative charges at each one, so it could be costly to open up too many accounts. The problem often arises if you hear of a good IRA investment which your broker can't sell because his firm doesn't handle the product. Nor will his firm let you buy from another broker and then transfer the securities. In this case, you may have to invest through the other broker and set up a separate IRA with his firm. Also, some self-directed IRAs may only allow the purchase of one or two specific securities, such as limited partnership offerings from only one sponsor. Unless there are no fees involved, avoid them as being too restrictive.

Wherever possible, you should try to merge IRA accounts. For example, some trustees will purchase no-load mutual funds for your IRA. Rather than create another IRA with the mutual fund's custodial bank, have one of your existing IRA trustees purchase the shares. You save the small administrative charges that the fund imposes. Another advantage is that you get one portfolio statement covering all your investments, which makes it easier to track them. And your dividends get swept into one IRA money market fund instead of two.

If you set up your self-directed IRA with a brokerage firm that is registered with the Securities and Exchange Commission as a broker/dealer, your account will be insured with the Securities Investor Protection Corporation (SIPC) for up to $500,000 in securities and up to $100,000 in cash. This is added protection in case the broker/dealer gets into financial difficulty.

With an independent trustee or custodian, you get no SIPC coverage, but the need is not as great because these companies aren't risking their own capital by taking positions in the securities markets, nor are they putting up your securities as collateral for loans. However, check with the trust company to be sure it has adequate insurance (usually a blanket fidelity bond) with a private insurer.

As might be expected, trustees and custodians charge a variety of fees for the establishment and maintenance of self-directed accounts.

The three basic IRA fees are the initial set-up fee, the annual maintenance fee, and the termination fee.

The initial set-up fee can range from $25 to $50. It goes toward processing the paperwork for establishing your account and entering relevant data into the trustee's computer. It also pays the costs of filing your plan adoption trust agreement. The annual maintenance fee pays for the trustee's work in collecting interest and dividend payments on your IRA investments, safekeeping of securities, making withdrawals and rollovers, accepting new contributions and reporting to the grantor and the IRS pertinent IRA information on a periodic basis. The termination fee goes toward the cost of closing the account, taking the information off the computer and storing it, and making a final report and accounting to the grantor and the IRS. However, termination fees are often waived in the event of disability, death, or retirement.

Percentage-wise, a maintenance fee of $35 a year for a $2,000 self-directed account is 1.75%. This could eat up a lot of your return. However, for a $10,000 IRA, the percent drops down to 0.35%. And for a $25,000 account, the $35 annual fee is only 0.14% of the assets. Therefore, annual fees for the larger accounts should have only a minor impact on overall portfolio performance.

When analyzing the self-directed fees charged by the various financial institutions, be sure to watch for those who charge annual administrative fees based on the amount of assets in the account. The fee charged is a percentage of the assets, calculated monthly, quarterly or annually. For example, a sliding scale fee schedule based on a percentage of assets might look like this:

Value of Account	*Percent of Assets*
Asset Value up to $ 10,000	1.0%
$ 10,001–$ 75,000	0.4 in excess of $ 10,000
$ 75,001–$150,000	0.3 in excess of $ 75,000
$150,001 and over	0.15 in excess of $150,000

These fees can add up rather quickly as your account grows, so try to avoid trustees and custodians with this type of compensation arrangement. Also stay away from those firms that charge a percentage of assets as a termination fee. Often they start at 1% of asset value but have a maximum charge for large accounts. In addition, watch out for trustees and custodians that levy a fee for each transaction. Some allow you a predetermined number of transactions per year, say five, and then impose a transaction charge. Fortunately, you shouldn't have a problem with this unless you do a lot of trading.

If you're not careful, you could be hit with almost $100 in fees for establishing a simple $2,000 IRA. For instance, one custodian charges a basic fee of $25, a special one-time fee of $10, quarterly variable fees totaling $16.80 for the year, and a quarterly regular fee of $10 ($40 annually). And if you make a special request of the custodian, such as a portfolio valuation for a divorce, you'll be billed $75 an hour. With this custodian, you can easily get nickeled and dimed to death in fees.

Some brokerage firms don't collect fees. They give away the IRA service and hope to make money from the commissions charged in buying and selling investments for the self-directed account holder. Beware of new firms or independent trustees that start out charging low fees; they may lure you in with this bait, but there's nothing to prevent them from raising fees some time down the road as long as they give you advance notification. And then you could be hit with a large termination fee if you decide to switch your self-directed account to a less expensive firm.

The table on the following page illustrates fees charged by a variety of the larger brokerage (full service and discount) firms and other companies in the IRA trustee/custodial business. Naturally, these are subject to change at any time.

As far as commissions are concerned, just about everyone charges a minimum of $35 per trade, although discounters may not charge quite as much. On larger trades, the commissions at full-service brokerage firms are up to 50% more than those of the discounters. Independent trustees don't execute orders; they must be handled by a broker/dealer through the trustee. Discounters usually limit the investment selection to stocks and bonds, whereas full service brokers and independent trustees usually offer the widest variety of investment selection (see Appendix E for a list of discount brokers).

Don't be afraid to negotiate IRA commissions, especially if you're a good customer. Commissions on limited partnerships and new issues will be fixed, but charges on secondary market transactions can be negotiated, especially if you have a regular brokerage account that's fairly active.

	Set-up	Admin	% Assets	Termination
Full Service Brokers				
Drexel Burnham	25	35 min.	.1%*	25
E.F. Hutton	0	25	None	0
INVEST (bank affiliate)	25	25	None	0
Merrill Lynch	0	20	None	0
Paine Webber	25	25	None	0
Prudential-Bache	0	24	None	50
Shearson Lehman	0	25	None	50
Discount Brokers				
Charles Schwab	0	0	None	0
Norstar Brokerage Corp.	25	25	None	50
Quick & Reilly	25	25	None	25
Independents				
Delaware Charter	25	35	None	50
First Trust Corporation	25	35	1%*	1% of assets up to $250
Retirement Accounts	25	42.50	None	50
Trust Company of America	25	50	.4%** plus $20 per order	1% of assets up to $30

* Maximum of $150
** Scaled down for large accounts

In addition to examining fees and commissions, you should also try to get a feeling for the type of service offered by the custodian or trustee. The best thing to do is to ask your broker or financial planner for customer references. Check with other IRA holders who use the trustee. Do they have an "800" telephone number which you can call to ask specific questions about your account? Has the trustee been responsive, do the employees know their jobs, do they provide accurate periodic portfolio statements, and do they give competent advise on what you can and can't do with your IRA?

Dealing with financial institutions can sometimes be frustrating. You'll want to minimize the pain and agony by chosing a good one. Stockbrokers will naturally push you in the direction of their firm's custodian, someone they're already familiar with. Your financial advisor will probably recommend one that he's had good experience with, because he too wants to minimize customer complaints which detract from more productive work.

You should also make sure that your self-directed accounts have a money market fund into which excess cash can be swept. Most will have this feature. There should be no minimum account balance requirements, for you want every dollar working for you earning interest. This is particularly important when you're receiving cash distributions, dividends, and interest payments from your investments on a regular basis. When the money market account builds up to a reasonable size, it can be used to make additional investments when the right situation comes along.

Also find out how often statements are sent to IRA clients. An annual statement is a must. The best trustee services provide quarterly statements, regardless of activity in the account, and monthly if there has been some change in the account. Security valuations should also be included to enable you to measure performance.

Signing Up

After you've decided on a financial advisor (assuming you wish to use the services of one for your self-directed IRA) and made a trustee or custodian selection, you'll be ready to put your hard-earned IRA money to work. In addition to signing and dating the plan adoption agreement, you should name a beneficiary.

If you like, you may designate your financial advisor or broker to act as your representative in executing buy and sell orders for your self-directed IRA. You may also want to sign a telephone authorization form which allows you to make certain transaction requests for your account over the phone. You can send the funds to the self-directed account trustee or custodian without making a specific investment. They will be held in a money market account pending further instructions.

But before you make any investment decisions right away, continue on to the next chapter for some suggestions on how to go about setting goals and objectives and developing an investment strategy for your self-directed IRA.

CHAPTER 4

Setting Goals and Objectives

How people should invest their IRA funds depends on a variety of factors such as their age, amount of funds in the IRA, investments held outside the IRA, pension benefits that can be expected at retirement, and more subjective considerations such as investment preferences and willingness to assume risk. The chart below shows several of these factors interacting with one another to indicate how conservative or aggressive a self-directed IRA investor should be.

Age and Other Factors

Approach	*20-30*				*31-40*				*41-50*				*51-60*				*61-70*			
	A	*B*	*C*	*D*	*A*	*B*	*C*	*D*	*A*	*B*	*C*	*D*	*A*	*B*	*C*	*D*	*A*	*B*	*C*	*D*
Conservative								x				x	x			x	x	x		x
Moderately Aggressive				x		x			x	x				x					x	
Aggressive	x	x			x						x				x					
Very Aggressive			x				x													

A = other assets outside IRA
B = good pension benefits expected
C = both assets and pension
D = neither assets nor pension adequate

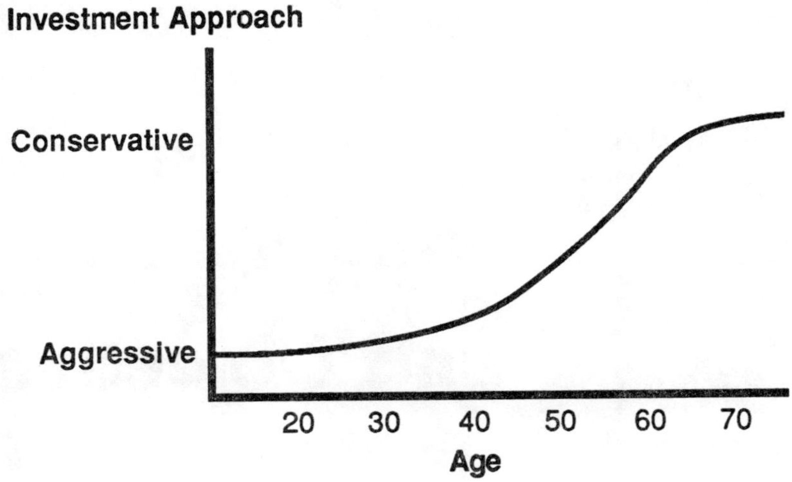

As you can see, the IRA investor starts out in his early years being fairly aggressive with his pension plan investments and eventually ends up in a conservative posture when retirement beckons. This evolutionary process is explained more fully below.

Age of IRA Owner

The IRA investor's age is one of the most critical factors in determining how a self-directed account will be handled. Usually, as a person matures his IRA as well as any outside investments will take on a more conservative color. He will become a more defensive investor. This life cycle process is depicted on the chart above.

Generally speaking, the young person will have only a small amount of assets relative to liabilities. These latter items may include a mortgage, a car loan, credit card debt, or even college loans that must be paid off. However, he knows that his discretionary income will grow over the years with salary increases. His financial priorities are to save funds to maintain some liquidity, satisfy the family need for life insurance, and eventually start an investment program.

He may or may not be interested in contributing to an IRA. However, not doing so at an early age may be a mistake. In addition to being a good tax deduction, the IRA can be used as a substitute for part of one's life and disability insurance needs, as well as an emergency fund during early adulthood. (However, it's not a dollar for dollar exchange because IRA withdrawals are taxed as ordinary income and life and disability insurance benefits are not usually taxed.) There's one other benefit: the 10% early withdrawal penalty won't apply to those persons under 59 and 1/2 who require IRA funds in the event of disability, or whose beneficiaries receive IRA distributions after the person dies.

The young IRA investor will probably want to be fairly aggressive in his approach to IRA investing. A few investment mistakes now can be made up for in later years. He has a long time horizon, with many years to go before retirement. Therefore, the young investor can take advantage of limited partnerships and growth funds, both of which need to be held for more than a few years to maximize returns.

Some young investors view their self-directed IRA funds as play money to speculate with. If they meet the eligibility requirements, then the IRA is more of a tax deduction than the beginnings of a retirement program. These persons reason that if they win big they won't have to pay taxes on the income. In addition, they can trade short-term without caring about tax consequences. If they lose some of the IRA money, so what—they would have paid part of it in taxes to Uncle Sam anyways.

A "dare to be great" investing attitude may pay off if the right bets are made. However, using this approach with an IRA may be a mistake. Constant trading usually will not be profitable in the long run—only the stockbroker's bank account will benefit. The commission costs are high when relatively few shares are traded, as most young persons will only have small IRAs. And very few persons can consistently beat the market by trading.

There's another penalty for taking too much risk. IRA losses cannot be deducted from adjusted gross income. If a young person has substantial assets outside his IRA, then it's better he use those assets to play the stock market. IRA funds should be placed in long-term, solid growth situations.

In many cases, a middle aged person will be at a point in his financial life where assets equal or exceed liabilities and his savings and insurance programs will be well underway. Often he's a member of a two-income family. He's probably in the process of raising children and his capital resources are starting to build into a small or medium-size net worth. However, a large part of savings may eventually go to pay the costs of college education for his children.

As his earnings and investments grow, the middle age person will be thinking about shifting income to other family members and using tax advantaged investments as a way to cut tax bills. His time horizon to retirement is still relatively long, say twenty years, but he's also beginning to think that preservation of capital is an important financial goal.

The middle aged person may still want to be somewhat aggressive with his self-directed IRA. He probably won't mind assuming greater risk if he's built up a sizable estate outside the IRA, or if he can count on a good pension at retirement. But basically, the middle aged person should stick with medium to high-yielding investments that won't burden him with too much risk.

By the time a person reaches middle age, he will have built up ten or more years of IRA contributions plus their earnings. This could amount to $30,000 to $40,000 or even more, depending on how well the IRA investments have performed. With this amount of funds to invest, the portfolio can be properly diversified, allowing for a slightly more aggressive investment posture.

A person in his fifties is in the home stretch, investing for his retirement years. Savings rates should be stepped up, with investments taking on a more conservative flavor.

The typical older person might be in late career or on the brink of retirement, which is no longer a vision or a dream, but a reality. He will want to sacrifice higher potential returns for lower-risk assets because the IRA carries great psychological weight.

Many older persons can ill afford to take losses in their IRAs. They will tend to invest quite conservatively. This doesn't mean they should stick all assets in a certificate of deposit when they reach age 59 and 1/2. It means that the mix of investments should gravitate toward the conservative side as one becomes older. The same would hold true for investments held outside an IRA. Protection of principal becomes important, because many people need the earning power of their IRA capital to live off of in retirement.

Those older persons who have a large outside income from a pension plan or other investments usually will not need to depend on the IRA for retirement income. They may plan to leave as much of the IRA as possible to their heirs as part of an estate. In these situations, the older person can afford to invest for growth to continue building an asset base.

Pension Plans and Other Assets

The self-directed IRA portfolio should be viewed as one part of a total retirement package, rather than in isolation. This includes expected Social Security and pension benefits, plus any other tax sheltered savings, profit-sharing, and retirement plans. The IRA owner must also consider the size and safety of all other assets on his balance sheet.

If a person holds substantial capital outside his IRA, or can count on a relatively sizable pension plan, he has more flexibility with the way in which he invests IRA funds. He can be more aggressive and reach for higher returns, knowing full-well that he's not totally dependent on the IRA for a comfortable retirement.

Persons who don't have additional assets or a good pension plan will have to be more careful with how they invest their IRA funds. They will move toward the more conservative side of the aisle and be content with high current yields backed by a reasonable degree of safety of principal.

One other factor should be considered. Unless a person's expected pension plan benefits increase in line with inflation, he may not be in as secure a position as he thinks when it comes to living a comfortable life during the golden years. If he expects to receive a fixed pension, then he may need to rely on the IRA for that extra boost in purchasing power to get over the hump.

Investment Experience

Persons with previous investment experience will no doubt open up self-directed IRA accounts rather than stash funds in savings bank CDs or in a money market mutual fund. They probably already have established a relationship with a broker, financial planner, or discount brokerage firm and have invested in stocks, bonds, limited partnerships or mutual funds. They are used to following their own judgment or that of an advisor in picking and chosing among the variety of investment alternatives available in the financial market place. Simply put, experienced investors are ripe for a self-directed IRA and all the benefits that accrue with it.

Other IRA investors may be reluctant to place their funds with someone they don't fully trust who puts it in an investment they don't understand. They may have only previously invested in the most conservative manner, either with a bank or a money market fund, or maybe even in a no-load mutual fund. They will either have to learn the investment game on their own or find an advisor whom they can trust. Otherwise they'll be relegated to the lower return, riskless investments that barely keep pace with inflation.

Some self-directed IRA investors will be motivated by the type of investments they're most familiar with or have had relative success with in the past. For example, a favorite investment may be real estate—something the IRA investor already knows about and is comfortable owning. Therefore, purchasing shares in a real estate investment trust won't be a difficult concept to understand. Or the person may have bought zero coupon bonds for his young son to help pay for the boy's college education. His familiarity with the bonds might motivate him to buy zeros for his IRA.

On the other hand, a person with a bad experience in a particular type of investment will very likely be turned off from investing his IRA in anything similar. However, this will limit his self-directed IRA investment choices, which could put a damper on total portfolio returns. This is unfortunate, because it's rare that a person makes the same error twice. Hopefully, everyone learns from his mistakes.

Risk Aversion

Then there's the question of the IRA investor's willingness to assume risk, also known as risk comfort level. This is very subjective notion and is based on a person's emotional temperment and attitudes. Some young investors may be very risk-oriented. It's their nature. They've never experienced a loss. Some older investors may also be willing to assume risk and go for high returns. But usually, as people get on in age they become more conservative in their invest-

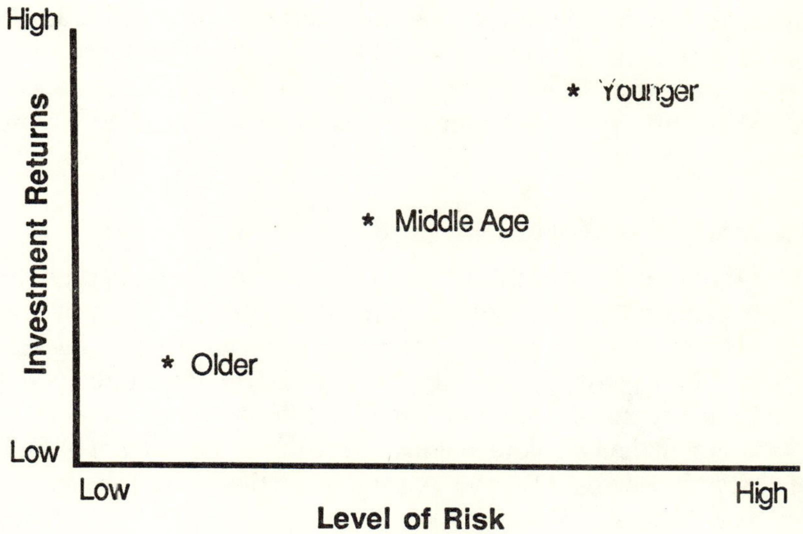

ment ways, as well as in their political and philosophical views on life.

It has been said that risk tolerance is based on a person's health, wealth, family situation, age, and temperment. All these factors come into play when he makes his investment decisions. As a person matures, his risk and reward trade-offs often change. The chart above depicts this phenomenon.

Whether a person is to the left or right of the point at his particular stage in life depends on his risk tolerance. If a person is to the left, then he's willing to assume less risk than the average person at that particular stage in life. Conversely, if the person is to the right, then he would be considered a risk taker.

The willingness to assume risk is also a function of the amount of funds at a person's disposal. Generally, the larger the net worth, the more a person is willing to assume risk. In this case, the person can afford to take risks with part of his funds because he can diversify better than other persons with not as many financial resources.

The purpose of the previous discussion was to point out that a person's investment attitudes depend on a variety of factors. How you fit into the IRA investment scheme is a very personal matter. You must assess your own situation and then set goals and objectives at the time you first open your self-directed IRA. If you already have an IRA, begin the process. The specific strategy you chose should govern what type of investments go into the account. Once you've established this, you can begin to make your self-directed IRA work for you.

Goals and Objectives

Both individual and institutional pension fund investors often find it difficult to articulate investment objectives with precision or consistency. The process involves a great deal of thought and soul-searching, but will ensure the development of a soundly conceived IRA investment program. Sometimes it's best done with a financial advisor who can articulate your feelings better than you can. The several goals listed below might serve as a good starting point for developing your own.

—High rate of return.
—Large real rate of return after inflation is taken into account.
—Maximum current income or yield.
—Preservation of capital.
—Minimal risk.
—Superior risk-adjusted rate of return.
—Rate of return higher than Treasury bill yields.
—Adequate liquidity.

Ideally, most IRA investors would like to have all of these statements as their personal goals. Unfortunately, some conflict with others. For instance, you cannot shoot for maximum returns while minimizing risk or preserving capital. One of the principle tenets of finance is that you can't have the surety of capital preservation without a low anticipated return. There have to be trade-offs among various goals. One way to deal with the problem of conflicting goals is to rank them or assign weights to them. This prioritization process will help sort out what is most important.

You should also establish some policy guidelines to follow in making your IRA investments. These could cover the type of investments that you want to consider, such as only stocks, no limited partnerships, no long-term bonds, or only stocks that are listed on an exchange. Also establish acceptable risk levels so that no more than a certain percent of the portfolio is invested in stocks, at least

$1,500 of liquid reserves is maintained, or minimum portfolio diversification requirements of at least six different investments at any one time are met.

Once you've established the broad outline of how you want to proceed, try to develop specific objectives that are quantified. This may appear to be going a bit too far, but it will serve to put you and your advisor on notice as to your exact expectations. The objectives must be consistent with your policy statements. You can't have a bond-only policy and expect to generate 15% returns when interest rates are only 10%, unless you expect bond prices to rise dramatically.

One interesting concept is to establish the amount of capital funds you think you will need at retirement, then work backwards to find a return that will get you there, assuming $2,000 annual contributions are made to your IRA. Use the chart in Appendix D, "the Magic of Compounding in an IRA." Assume you are 35 years old and plan to retire at 60 and hope to have $300,000 in your IRA at that time. Going to the chart, you'll discover that in order to reach that objective, you'll need to generate annual compound returns of 12%.

Examples of other specific IRA objectives are:

—Achieve a 10% annual compound growth rate over each five-year period.
—Beat inflation by 3% on average over a three-year period.
—Equity investments outperform stock market by not less than either 25% better than the S&P 500, or by two percentage points.
—Long-term bond investments should outperform the bond indicies by one percentage point.

With these objectives, you have something to compare IRA performance with that is specific. Either you accomplished them or you didn't. Chapter 10 will explain several methods to determine your self-directed IRA's performance. If it looks like your objectives were unrealistic, don't be afraid to alter them. Likewise, when your personal situation changes, the goals and objectives may need modification as circumstances warrant.

Now that you've developed your goals and objectives and your policy guidelines, the next step is to implement them by making good sound investments. Before describing some that are especially suitable for IRAs, several important investing strategies will be discussed in the next chapter.

CHAPTER 5

Two Important Investment Strategies for Self-Directed IRAs

After you've figured out your goals and objectives based on your individual circumstances and other relevant factors, you need to be mindful of two key investment strategies that will help you maximize the benefits to be derived from your self-directed IRA. These are the "current yield" strategy and the "inflation protection" strategy. The degree to which you implement one or both will depend on the goals and objectives you've chosen and your own personal situation. After reading this chapter, you might want to go back and reasses your IRA objectives to put more emphasis on these strategies.

Current Yield Strategy

The old familiar adage "a dollar today is worth more than a dollar tomorrow" clearly applies to individual retirement accounts. Early returns on an investment are always preferable to identical returns received at a later date. This is the same as saying that a bird in the hand's worth—you guessed it—two in the bush. The reason is simple. The dollar today is more certain than tomorrow's dollar. In addition, you can reinvest today's dollar, and that dollar plus interest earned will be worth more than if you received just the dollar a year from now. This is the same as the concept of present value, whereby future returns are discounted to their present worth using an appropriate interest rate.

Take the following example. A dollar today compounded annually for five years at 10% would be worth $1.61 at the end of that time. If you were offered $1.50 in five years, you should turn it down without question and take today's dollar, assuming you could invest it risk-free at a 10% or better rate for each of those five years. This is the magic of compound interest—interest continuously earning interest.

The dollar today concept is even more applicable to IRAs because earnings compound tax free within the account. Also, trade-offs between future capital gains and current income are not beneficial in IRAs because each is taxed at the same rate when funds are withdrawn. Another reason why it's better to have your money today rather than tomorrow is that build-ups of current cash flow within your self-directed IRA can be used to take advantage of profitable new investment opportunities as they materialize. A final reason is that if one of your IRA investments goes sour and you're in danger of losing part or all of your capital, at least you've recouped a portion of your investment in the form of high current yields.

With better than average cash flows from interest, dividends and other distributions, the IRA account begins to build up at a quick rate. That's because no taxes are paid on the earnings until they are eventually drawn out. The magic of compounding is working all the more for you when your reinvestment rate quickens. The faster you put those cash flows to work, the faster they compound. This can be demonstrated through the use of the following table, which shows the difference between annual and quarterly compounding:

$2,000 Invested With Earnings Compounded Quarterly and Annually at Several Interest Rates

	5%		*10%*		*15%*	
	Qtly.	*Ann.*	*Qtly.*	*Ann.*	*Qtly.*	*Ann.*
Year 1	$2102	$2100	$2208	$2200	$2317	$2300
2	2209	2205	2437	2420	2685	2645
3	2322	2315	2690	2662	3103	3042

As this example shows, the higher the yield, the larger the difference in account build-up between quarterly and annual compounding. At 15%, you get two per cent more after only three years; but on interest alone (subtracting the initial $2,000), the difference is almost 6%. This spread gets larger as the years roll on. And they'd be even higher if daily or monthly compounding rates were used in the example.

Although it's nice to realize capital gains in your IRA as the investments mature, such income is taxed the same as ordinary income when funds are withdrawn. As far as IRA tax benefits are concerned, there's no special distinction between capital gain and ordinary income.

In general, most IRA investors should not take additional risk to shoot for capital gains at the expense of giving up high current returns. It's better to hold these investments outside your IRA, where gains will be taxed at more favorable rates. Capital gains are usually riskier to come by and that's why they get preferential tax treatment. In addition, if you take the extra risk in your self-directed IRA and end up with losses, you can't deduct them. But if you incur losses on investments held outside your IRA, then you can deduct them against other income on your tax returns.

It's better to go for slow, steady returns in IRAs, rather then assume much greater risk for the possibility of higher reward. The following example demonstrates why "slow and steady" often wins the IRA race. Assume a $2,000 investment earns 15% a year returns, but one year there is a 10% loss of capital. Compare the results to a steady 10% a year return with no losses. Incidentally, both streams of returns add up to a 50% gain over the period—15% times 4 minus 10% for the first, versus 10% times 5 for the second.

End of Year:	*15% Return With One Loss in Two Different Years*		*10% Return With No Losses*
1	$2300	$2300	$2200
2	2070*	2645	2420
3	2381	3042	2662
4	2738	2738*	2928
5	3148	3148	3221

* 10% loss of capital in this year.

The results show the steady 10% return winning the race by about 3.7%. It's not a huge percentage, but is still meaningful on a large dollar amount. And over a longer timespan, those are lost dollars not at work compounding in your IRA.

As your cash flow builds up from high-yielding investments, you can store them in a money market fund until the right opportunity comes along to make another good investment. In other words, you'll always have reserve funds to take advantage of special situations.

For instance, if you own mutual funds or individual stocks and the market heads south, you can purchase more shares and average down if you have extra funds available. Or if interest rates go up, you'll have cash to take advantage of higher-yielding securities. Simply put, high current yields from IRA investments mean more flexibility in making new investments or adding to existing ones.

Finally, with high current returns you're assured of getting some part of your investment back as quickly as possible. The increased volatility of the stock and bond markets in recent years makes high cash flows even more desirable. This is an important consideration when viewing long-term investments, particularly those that are illiquid such as limited partnerships. If you wait for capital gains and they don't materialize, then you're out the opportunity cost of not having the funds earn income elsewhere. With high current yields, you don't have to worry as much about winning the capital gain game.

Naturally you'll want to be wary of yields that are out of line with the rest of the market, for there's always a reason for this. Although not perfect, the financial markets continually reflect investor perceptions of risk and reward. Information travels freely and there aren't that many undervalued situations at any one point in time. This is known as the efficient market concept. Therefore, extraordinarily high yields on a security often raise a red flag that the dividends or interest payments are not secure. Remember, higher returns beget higher risks.

The value of any investment is based on the expected flow of future returns, their certainty, and their timing. The higher and quicker the returns, the more expensive the investment. In the case of bonds, the returns are interest payments; in the case of stocks they're dividends; and for real estate, they're rents.

The bond market places a premium on high current returns. For a given change in interest rates, lower coupon bonds are more volatile than high coupon bonds. That's because the average time to complete repayment is further out in the future for lower coupon bonds, so there's more impact on price from discounting future cash flows. The table below illustrates this concept:

	Coupon	Years to Maturity	Interest Rate Level 8% Price	Interest Rate Level 7% Price	Per Cent Change
Bond "A"	8%	20yrs	100.000	110.677	10.7
Bond "B"	4%	20yrs	60.414	67.967	12.5

When interest rate levels changed, the 8% bond moved less than the 4% bond did (10.7% versus 12.5%). Less volatility equates with higher current interest payments.

Another example using common stocks shows why it's often better to receive current income than to speculate on sometimes ephemeral capital gains. Company A's stock—considered a growth stock—currently yields only 2%, but its dividend is growing at 10% a year. Company B's stock—classified as an income stock—is now yielding a generous 7%, but that dividend is only increasing at a 2% annual rate. Surprisingly, it will take seventeen years before A's total dividend payments reach the sum of B's. That's a long time to breakeven with a stock that is presumably more risky in the first place because of its higher growth rate.

Fortunately for self-directed IRA owners, there is little evidence that the preponderance of investors in today's stock market are solely interested in high yields. Periodically there's talk of movement in that direction. This may happen when institutional investment results are poor because the pros have taken a beating chasing high growth stocks. Also, during periods of increased economic uncertainty many investors take a defensive position in higher-yielding stocks. Other than during these short-term phenomena, there's still plenty of opportunities for self-directed IRA investors to put assets in high-yield securities without paying premium prices for them.

Protecting Against Inflation

Although inflation has dropped to near zero from the double-digit numbers of several years ago, it's still a very real threat to the purchasing power of the retirement dollar. Even at a relatively low rate of 5%, inflation will cause the value of a dollar to drop by 40% in as little as ten years. At 7% inflation, the value declines by almost half during that same timespan. Regrettably, this latter figure is about the average U.S. inflation rate for the last decade.

Another bit of history is also worth contemplating. In 1971, with prices rising at only 3.2%, the country was in a panic about runaway inflation. As a result, President Nixon imposed wage and price controls on the U.S. economy. Hopefully, Americans have not grown too complacent fifteen years later.

Advertisements for IRAs often show the dramatic growth in funds attributable to investing IRA dollars at different rates of return. Huge sums of $1 million or more could be amassed in a person's lifetime if he earned medium to high double-digit returns on yearly contributions. This is made possible through the magic of compounding and the fact that earnings accrue on a tax-deferred basis.

Unfortunately, inflation benefits from these same forces at work. Its deleterious effect on the purchasing power of your dollar compounds tax-free. Each year's inflation rate is keyed off the previous year's base, which seems to rise inexorably. And because the rate is derived from a package of consumer goods and services, it's calculated on an after-tax basis. So if your IRA grows to a million dollars in thirty years, then a loaf of bread will run you $4.32 in 2015, based on today's cost of $1.00 and a 5% inflation rate.

How can an IRA investor protect his portfolio against inflation? Not too long ago, the financial pundits recommended putting money into such hard assets as real estate, oil and gas, diamonds, gold and silver, stamps and coins, and even antique furniture and art. When the inflation rate exceeded double-digit figures twice in the last ten years (hitting an incredible 13.5% in 1980), the prices of tangibles increased dramatically. Individuals went on a speculative binge and bid prices up even further, reminiscent of the Dutch Tulip Bulb bubble in the 1600's. Of course, other factors at work accounted for price increases—the Arab oil embargo, the strength of the building cycle, and weak stock and bond markets, not to mention investor "follow the herd" psychology.

Prices of hard assets have cooled down in the last few years, as evidenced by the figures in the Salomon Brothers chart shown below. Returns from financial assets such as stocks and bonds have done much better in recent years, particularly 1985 and the first half of 1986.

The notion of investing in hard assets as an inflation hedge lost its appeal when prices of oil, gas, precious metals, and other commodi-

Compounded Annual Rates of Return

	15 Years	*Rank*	*10 Years*	*Rank*	*5 Years*	*Rank*	*1 Year*	*Rank*
Oil[a]	19.7%	1	8.0%	9	(5.4)%	12	(4.5)%	10
U.S. Coins	17.7	2	20.4	1	0.1	9	11.5	4
Gold	15.5	3	6.9	13	(11.0)	14	(20.3)	14
Chinese Ceramics[b]	14.3	4	17.1	2	1.0	8	5.9	6
Stamps	14.1	5	14.5	3	0.1	10	(9.6)	11
Diamonds	10.4	6	9.5	7	1.2	7	0.0	9
Old Masters[b]	9.1	7	10.7	4	1.5	6	13.6	3
Treasury Bills	9.1	8	10.0	6	12.0	3	9.5	5
Bonds	8.7	9	9.3	8	13.2	2	42.9	1
Silver	8.7	10	3.5	14	(15.9)	15	(34.3)	15
Stocks	8.5	11	10.4	5	15.2	1	28.7	2
U.S. Farmland	8.5	12	6.9	12	(1.7)	11	(10.0)	12
Housing	8.2	13	7.9	10	4.3	5	2.5	8
CPI	**7.1**	**14**	**7.3**	**11**	**5.7**	**4**	**3.7**	**7**
Foreign Exchange	2.0	15	(0.6)	15	(7.9)	13	(11.3)	13

Inflation Scorecard (Number of Assets That Outperformed Inflation)

	15 Years	10 Years	5 Years	1 Year
Tangibles	10 out of 10	7 out of 10	0 out of 10	3 out of 10
• Collectibles	4 out of 4	4 out of 4	0 out of 4	3 out of 4
• Commodities	4 out of 4	2 out of 4	0 out of 4	0 out of 4
• Real Estate	2 out of 2	1 out of 2	0 out of 2	0 out of 2
Financials	3 out of 4	3 out of 4	3 out of 4	3 out of 4

[a] Reflects revision in oil index.
[b] Source: Sotheby's.
Note: All returns are for the period ended June 1, 1985, based on latest available data.
SOURCE: Salomon Brothers, Inc.

ties dropped during the early 1980s. However, the prospect for moderate inflation is still a reality, and IRA investors should try and take steps to cope with it as best they can. Thanks to large Federal budget deficits, lower exchange rates for the dollar, and easier credit, double digit inflation could very well rear its ugly head again. Fortunately, self-directed IRA investors have the ability to insulate their portfolios against the ravages of this destroyer of the retirement nest egg.

IRA rules prohibit direct investments in collectibles, real estate, commodities, precious metals and other hard assets. But this doesn't necessarily rule out the possibility of indirectly investing in these assets. There are real estate partnerships and investment trusts, gold and silver mining company stocks, and oil and gas company stocks, income partnerships, and royalty trusts that the IRA investor can legally include in his portfolio. Self-directed account holders have the flexibility to pick from a range of choices. The ultimate selection will be determined by individual investing preferences and tolerance for risk.

Real estate has been called the traditional inflation hedge, the notion being that as the consumer price index rises, rents can be increased to offest the costs of owning property. And relatively high operating margins will generate greater cash flows, which in turn mean greater property values. When capital gains are added in, total returns from real estate ownership could outpace inflation by a considerable amount. Some investors argue that real estate holds its value over the long term despite fluctuating interest rates, weak financial markets, and inflation.

This theory has worked well in the past and could repeat itself. But remember, the value of an investment property today is a function of the future income it will produce. As investors in the city of Houston, Texas, and a few other oil-dependent cities know all too well, supply and demand for commercial and residential space impacts heavily on the rents that can be charged. Where there is an imbalance, rents can indeed slip backwards.

The most suitable real estate investments for IRAs are income-oriented. Simply put, they do not employ leverage, but have 100% equity ownership in the properties they buy. All cash flows generated are paid out to limited partners or shareholders. Income-oriented real estate has the advantage of high current returns and some capital gain; as was stated before, a dollar received today in an IRA is worth more than a dollar collected tomorrow. And high yields compound on a tax-deferred basis, adding grow power to your account.

It's also possible to buy leveraged real estate for your IRA to protect against hyper-inflation. This technique will magnify returns if the properties go up in value. With leverage in a limited partnership or real estate investment trust, you'll get little or no current income for the first several years. In fact, you lose the tax benefits they offer because partnership losses can't be deducted in an IRA. (As will be explained later, however, the losses can be used to offset any unrelated business taxable income greater than $1,000 in your IRA.)

With leveraged real estate, you're banking solely on capital gain. The reason is that for every equity dollar at stake, there are two to three borrowed dollars working for you. As the value of the property goes up, your equity investment increases at double or triple that rate. Leveraged real estate could provide an excellent hedge against inflation, assuming the right properties are bought. But with greater potential returns come higher risks—if the value of the real estate decreases, your equity can quickly disappear.

The biggest drawback with real estate is that it is a comparatively illiquid investment. It needs to be held for the long term to maximize returns. Happily, this approach is consistent with the objectives of an IRA program. You're not in it to be trading short-term. But even if you insist on investing for the short or medium-term, you can purchase relatively liquid shares of real estate investment trusts for your IRA portfolio, as explained in Chapter 6 of this book.

Another popular investment for those worried about the prospects for hyper-inflation is gold and silver. Although gold and silver cannot be directly held in an IRA, you can get a piece of this action indirectly through the purchase of stock in a mining company or through a gold mutual fund. If inflation kicks up and there's a flight to gold, then these stocks should do well. As the price of precious metals increases, mining companies profits surge because of their high operating margins once fixed costs have been covered. Some of the South African gold mines pay fairly good current dividends, although the political situation there presents considerable investment risk. The North American mining companies pay little or no dividends, but you can purchase convertible bonds of one company, Sunshine Mining Company, which are exchangable for silver bullion bars.

Oil and gas investments are another former favorite of the inflation fighters. However, the prices of these commodities now appear to be very closely tied to free-market supply and demand. As everyone knows, the Arabs are no longer in control of their own destiny, so prices of these natural resources have been in a deflationary, rather than inflationary trend. Nevertheless, some IRA investors with a long time horizon may want to keep a portion of their funds in carefully selected oil and gas income or royalty programs, as over time the current oil glut will in all likelihood disappear.

Oil and gas programs pay fairly high current returns at the expense of lower asset values down the road. Some of the distributions are what is known in the securities industry as a return of capital. In other words, unless new reserves are discovered, or the price of oil increases dramatically, your IRA investment will probably decline in value over a period of years.

With a self-directed IRA, you can buy stocks of companies in the fields of natural resources, basic commodities and other hard assets. You can also buy mutual funds which specialize in investing in these companies. Funds such as the Fidelity Resources Sector Fund or the T.Rowe Price New Era Fund have most of their assets invested in the stocks of natural resource companies. If commodity prices turn upwards and increase at a rate greater than inflation, then the stocks of these companies could respond favorably to the prospects of greater profits.

Another concern for those wishing to protect their IRA assets against inflation is investing in the equities and fixed income markets. It wasn't too many years ago that economic and financial experts were espousing the ownership of common stocks as the best way to beat inflation. The thinking was that corporate managers could index profits to changes in inflation rates. Therefore, if corporations could raise prices and increase profits, the prices of their stocks would move up. But that was when inflation was at very managable levels—averaging two or three percentage point increases a year—and the stock market was performing rather well.

Up until the early 1970s, the average returns for common stocks had been about 9% annually, which was much better than the low inflation rates experienced in days past. However, the last decade proved that common stocks were no match for inflation, as depreciation schedules failed to compensate for higher asset replacement costs and corporate profits eroded. As everyone now knows, few business have been able to protect their profit margins in inflationary times.

The type of stocks to purchase for your self-directed IRA in an inflationary economy are shares of companies that can raise prices easily and pass on increased costs to their customers. Also benefiting will be those corporations with low labor and commodity costs as a percent of total costs. If the prices of these components move up, variable costs will not be affected significantly, and these companies will be able to maintain and possibly increase profit margins.

The erosion of principal for fixed income investors is another problem caused by inflation. When inflationary times push interest rates up, the prices of bonds fall. The real rate of interest is what investors are willing to pay to rent money, not counting an inflation premium. For example, when inflation is at 2% and long-term interest rates are at 8%, then the real rate of interest is 6%. If inflation accelerates to 10%, and the real rate stays at 6%, then interest rates will have to rise to 16%. If this scenario materializes, the subsequent drop in bond prices would be severe. Fixed income investors remember this is exactly what happened not too long ago.

There is also an inflation expectation factor built into the level of interest rates that can keep rates high even though inflation is low. This occurs when people believe that low inflation is only a temporary phenomenon. If the rate of inflation is expected to accelerate in the future, long-term securities will be less attractive and investors will sell them. Bond prices will drop and yields will increase to compensate for inflation expectations.

Those self-directed IRA investors who are concerned about the prospects for future inflation will probably want to stay with short to medium-term debt instruments carrying relatively high coupon rates. This will serve several purposes. First of all, if inflation and interest rates do rise, you won't lose as much of your principal if you have to liquidate. Second, if you don't want to realize a capital loss, then you can hold the instruments to maturity without a long wait to collect their face value. Third, if you buy long-term bonds and guess wrong, you may decide to sell them for a capital loss, rather than sit with them forever. However, as was pointed out before, you can't deduct these IRA losses from your income.

It's still possible to generate higher than money market yields in your self-directed IRA and at the same time insulate the fixed income portion of your portfolio against the vagaries of adverse interest rate movements. Purchase two relatively unknown securities—variable rate preferred stocks and put bonds.

Variable rate preferreds have been popular when interest rates were high and banks and corporations were trying to save a few basis points on the cost of raising capital. Several of these preferred stocks trade on the New York Stock Exchange. The dividend rate is adjusted periodically in concert with some well known interest rate barometer such as the average yield on 90-day Treasury bills or on a five-year note. The rate is also subject to a collar, where it cannot fall outside a minimum and maximum level.

As might be expected, the variability of the interest rate assures that the price of the preferred stock will not move up or down significantly. Therefore, if interest rates increase, the dividend will be adjusted upward and the price of the stock should stay relatively stable.

The "put" bond is another new type of fixed income investment phenomenon that appears suitable for self-directed IRAs. They are issued with maturities of ten years, but somewhere along the way, the bondholder has the option of selling the bond back to the issuer at par. Thus the name put bond.

If interest rates rise at the end of five years, then it's to the advantage of the put bond holder to cash them in and use the proceeds to buy higher yielding securities. On the other hand, if interest rates are down at the end of this period, presumably the investor will hold the bonds until they mature. There are two drawbacks to be concerned with: the bonds are usually issued by companies of medium-grade investment quality, and the smallest denomination is $5,000, thus making them only suitable for large IRAs.

As you have seen, there are many ways to insulate your IRA portfolio against inflation. With the self-directed account, you have the flexibility to invest in a variety of securities to meet your inflation-fighting objectives as you build your retirement nest egg. In the following chapter, other investments suitable for your IRA are discussed.

CHAPTER 6

Investments Designed for Self-Directed IRAs

A variety of investments make excellent choices for self-directed IRAs, depending on one's objectives, tolerance for risk, and investment preferences. The more appropriate ones are presented in this chapter.

Many are oriented toward the current yield side of the financial fence, which should fit in well with the goals and objectives of most IRA owners. These securities are neither extremely conservative nor highly speculative. Included in this investment review is a recent invention, the zero coupon bond, as well as the more traditional mutual funds. Rounding out the choices are limited partnerships, certain higher yielding stocks, real estate investment trusts, and other types of equity equivalents such as convertible bonds and preferred stocks. (Lists of limited partnerships and mutual funds that may be suitable for self-directed IRAs are found in Appendices A and B, respectively.)

Certain securities usually make poor candidates for IRA investments. These include anything that has a tax advantage, such as discount bonds, tax shelters, and tax-exempt securities. Putting them in your IRA is analagous to wearing suspenders and a belt at the same time. These securities duplicate functions, because an IRA is already tax sheltered; you don't gain any benefits with the extra tax break. Simply put, most tax advantaged investments should be held outside your IRA, where they can be put to maximum use.

As explained previously, most capital gain-oriented investments should also be kept away from the IRA umbrella. You can't take advantage of the lower capital gains tax rate inside the IRA—all income is taxed at ordinary rates when it's eventually withdrawn. If you have a preponderance of pure growth securities in your IRA and are holding income investments on the outside, then the two should be "exchanged" to minimize taxes. (Regretably, IRA rules require that the IRA investments be sold for cash and then reinvested in new securities.)

One additional caveat: any self-directed IRA owner who can't understand an investment shouldn't be in it unless he relies on the expertise and judgment of competent financial advisors. You should be particularly careful of investments that appear too sophisticated and complicated to easily comprehend, for these are often the most risky. Nonetheless, the more alternatives you learn about, the more informed choices you'll have for making self-directed IRA investments.

Zero Coupon Bonds

Zero coupon bonds have become a favorite investment medium for owners of self-directed IRAs. Several reasons easily explain this phenomenon. In the first place, the bonds are sold in small $1,000 denominations as opposed to the usual $5,000 lot size. Secondly, interest payments are automatically "reinvested" at the same rate every six months, so there's no problem of recycling your interest income. Thirdly, there isn't any worry about having the bonds called prematurely, for no issuer in his right mind is going to pay par for a deeply discounted bond. Fourthly, investors like the idea of paying a very low price for the bonds. A $1,000 bond can be purchased for as little as $150 to $200—it sounds like the road to instant wealth. Finally, although most persons are taxed for imputed interest on zeros, IRA and other tax-exempt investors don't have this problem with phantom income.

As the name implies, zero coupon bonds have no stated interest rate and pay no current interest. Instead, they're sold at a discount from par and the bondowner receives 100% of par value at maturity. The bonds are treated by the IRS as original discount bonds, whereby the annual accretion (also known as imputed interest) is considered to be taxable income to those bondholders who pay taxes.

Theoretically, the value of the zero coupon bond increases each year as it reaches maturity and is finally paid off at face value. This is the same concept used by the Federal government for U.S. savings bonds and Treasury bills. For example, a ten-year bond sold at $463 yields 8% to maturity (using annual, not semi-annual compounding), and will increase in value as follows, assuming no change in the general level of interest rates during this time period:

Year	*Annual Increase*	*Year-end Value*
0	$ 0	$ 463
1	37	500
2	40	540
3	43	583
4	47	630
5	51	681
6	54	735
7	59	794
8	63	857
9	69	926
10	74	1000

The extent of the discount on a zero coupon bond and the number of years to maturity determine its yield. The yield to maturity is the same as the semi-annual compounding rate. Corporate and U.S. government zeros are most appropriate for IRAs because they have higher yields than tax-exempt zeros and, as was explained before, IRA owners don't need the benefit of this type of income.

The chart below depicts various yields to maturity and the time it takes to double, triple, and quadruple your money with a zero coupon bond. It doesn't take very long to accomplish this, especially at the higher yields. That's the magic of compounding working for your self-directed IRA.

The first zero coupon bonds were issued by corporations back in the early 1980s. One problem encountered in marketing them was that there were no guarantees that the corporation would be around in twenty to thirty years to make good on the bonds when they matured. The investor might lose not only the principal, but also all of the

Yield to Maturity*	Period Required for $1,000 to: Double	Triple	Quadruple
7	10/3	16/3	20/6
8	9/0	14/3	18/0
9	8/0	12/9	16/1
10	7/1	11/3	14/2

* Annual compounding assumed
** Years/months

deferred interest payments. (Remember, a dollar today is worth. . . .)

In 1982, some clever folks on Wall Steet discovered they could manufacture zero coupon bonds backed by the full faith and credit of the U.S. government. They did this by separating the interest and principal payments for various maturities of government bonds and placing them in a custodial account with a bank. The security of these bonds stood behind the reciepts and certificates that were sold to the public as zero coupon bonds. The most popular came to be known as CATS (Certificates of Accrual on Treasury Securities), which were developed by Salomon Brothers or TIGRs (Treasury Investment Growth Receipts), created by Merrill Lynch.

Then the Treasury Department discovered that due to the popularity of zeros, their yields were slightly lower than those on its comparable straight bonds. Therefore, the Treasury decided it could cut its borrowing costs by issuing its own version known as STRIPS (Separate Trading of Registered Interest and Principal of Securities). These Treasury zeros represent the direct ownership of future principal and interest payments on U.S. Treasury bonds. STRIPS are also based on the zero coupon concept: they pay no semiannual interest, but sell at a deep discount and pay full face value upon maturity.

STRIPS yield slightly less than TIGRs and CATS because they're perceived as safe as direct obligations of the United States Treasury. With the other zeros, owners are one step removed from actual ownership of the bonds, even though they're held in irrevocable trust with custodian banks.

Zero coupon bonds are sold in denominations of $1,000 and maturity dates of every year out for the next thirty years or so. There's a wide variety to chose from. CATS, bank, and corporate zeros trade on the New York Stock Exchange and others trade in the over-the-counter market. Generally speaking, the corporates yield three quar-

1985 Total Returns Based on Present Term Structure*

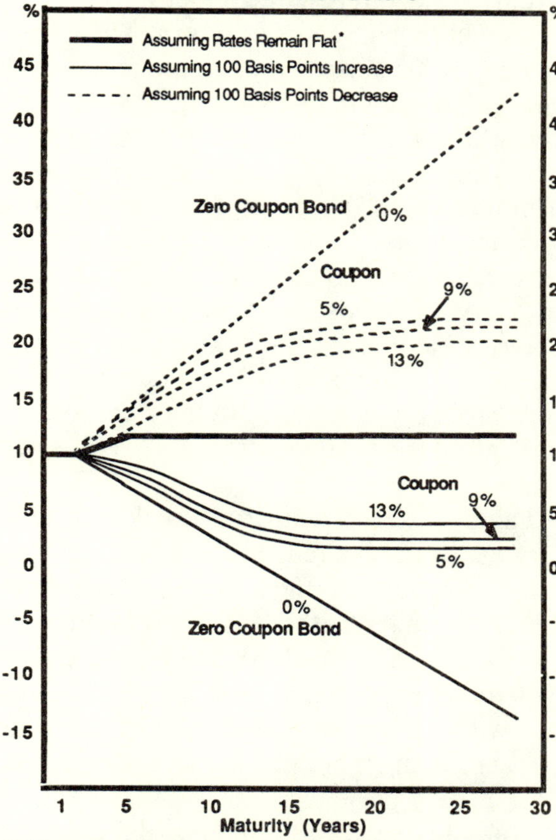

* Allows for shortening of maturities in portfolios.
This chart illustrates that as interest rates change, a zero coupon bond is more volatile in its price movement than a coupon bond.
Source: *Bank Credit Analyst*, BCA Publications Ltd., 1985.

ters to a full one per cent more than Treasury-backed securities. Maturities can be purchased to coincide with when you will eventually be withdrawing funds from your self-directed IRA.

As many investors are discovering, zeros are much more volatile than regular coupon bonds. Price swings of 20%, either up or down, can occur in fifteen-year bonds with only a two per cent change in long-term interest rate levels. The chart above demonstrates this volatility if interest rates move up and down by only one percentage point.

As previously mentioned, zeros pay no interest so you don't have the problem of reinvesting interest at competitive market rates. If you buy right, you can lock in high rates of return. This is helpful for self-directed IRA investors, because normally the money market rates at which you might temporarily invest your interest payments from medium to long-term bonds will be lower. For smaller IRAs with low streams of current income, only money market rates are available until idle cash builds up to the point that a large purchase can be made. This problem is solved with zero coupon bonds.

The biggest drawback to zero coupon bond investing is that if rates go up after you buy your bonds, you lose two ways. First, you can't reinvest your interest income at those higher rates because you're not getting cash payments. Therefore, when you believe interest rates will go up, you're probably better off buying a corporate bond mutual fund, where current interest payments can be reinvested in the fund at higher rates.

Second, the value of zeros will drop quickly in response to the higher interest rates. For these reasons, it's best not to get lured into buying long-term zero coupon bonds, unless rates offered are unusually high. The shorter the term, the less the volatility. Even though a $2,000 IRA contribution may enable you to buy zeros with a maturity value of $15,000 in twenty years, you'll probably do better in a shorter maturity with a face value of only $5,000. In any event, be prepared to hold zero coupon bonds until maturity to realize their full potential.

One last thought. Check several broker/dealers for prices and yield to maturity, including sales commissions and other markups, before you buy zero coupon bonds. There's usually a wide variation in quotes on zeros from market-maker to market-maker. An advantage of having more than one self-directed IRA is that you're not locked into buying exclusively from one broker—you can shop price.

Mutual Funds

Although some IRA trustees/custodians restrict the purchase of mutual funds to certain funds (for example, load funds in the case of brokerage firms), they may also be purchased through an independent trustee or the mutual fund's own custodian. Mutual funds can play a key role in the make-up of a self-directed IRA portfolio, particularly in the first few years when it's still small.

Mutual funds are an alternative to investing your self-directed IRA funds directly in individual stocks and bonds. They provide a measure of diversification and professional money management not available to the average investor. Often, IRAs are too small to enable their holders to buy enough individual stocks and bonds to achieve adequate diversification to minimize risk. A $10,000 IRA would only allow for the purchase of a few bonds or stocks. In addition, acquiring very small quantities of securities (i.e., odd lots) increases transaction costs—the commissions and markups associated with buying and selling securities.

Mutual funds can be used either as a substitute for the purchase of individual stocks and bonds or as a supplement to them. Suppose you wanted to put part of your self-directed portfolio in high growth stocks, but were uncomfortable picking them yourself or having your advisor select them for you. Chosing a mutual fund which invested in a variety of these stocks would be the logical route to go. This would provide greater diversification to reduce the risk associated with the loss of capital on a single investment. In addition, with a mutual fund you won't have to spend a lot of time following highly volatile stocks and monitoring fast-changing industry developments; the fund managers do this for you.

Likewise, if you wanted to receive the benefits from a diversified group of straight corporate, convertible, or government bonds for your IRA portfolio, then this could be achieved more easily by purchasing a mutual fund that specialized in one of these bonds. You could buy into a mutual fund portfolio for as little as $500, whereas often the minimum purchase price for an individual bond is $1,000. And the commissions and markups on single bonds can be relatively high.

Most experienced investors know that a variety of mutual funds are available to holders of IRAs. Some funds are known as load because they have a sales charge, while most are no-load. Your financial advisor or stockbroker can help you pick a fund that is suitable for your needs. It can become the cornerstone of your portfolio, or serve the function of rounding it out by adding an element not easily available through direct investment.

The more appropriate mutual funds for most self-directed IRAs are those which are oriented toward the production of current income. Again, this is based on the notion of a dollar today being worth more than a dollar tomorrow, and the fact that current income is taxed no differently than capital gain income in an IRA. Fortunately, there are a variety of funds which fit this bill. They can be classified into growth-income funds, income funds and bond funds.

Growth-Income Funds

Growth-income funds attempt to give investors a reasonable return based on a combination of long-term capital appreciation and current income. The emphasis is on the word "long term." Most of their portfolios are in stocks which have higher than average yields compared to other types of mutual funds. This provides relative stability for an equity investment; although growth-income funds may be sluggish while the stock market is rising, they're not likely to drop as fast when the market is falling.

Several contrarian mutual funds fall into the growth-income category. They invest in out-of-favor stocks that nobody else wants. If the stocks rise in value, the funds sell them as they become more popular with other investors. The proceeds are used to invest in other depressed issues. The contrarian investment philosophy requires the fund advisors to have strength of conviction and patience for it to work.

Income Funds

Income funds, on the other hand, invest about half their assets in dividend paying stocks, and the balance in convertible or straight-debt securities and preferred stocks. Some specialize in high-yielding common stocks and convertible bonds, and are known as equity-income funds. They try to generate as much income as possible consistent with reasonable risk, but also have a secondary objective of capital appreciation. Option income funds seek high current returns by primarily investing in dividend paying common stocks and writing covered puts and call options on them. Income funds vary widely in portfolio composition, so you must look closely at the prospectus and latest list of holdings to determine exactly what you're investing in.

Bond Funds

It really doesn't make much sense to buy individual bonds for your self-directed portfolio (except for possibly convertible bonds), when you can find a bond fund that will meet your needs for relatively high income and some safety of principal. Bond funds provide instant diversification for a small IRA investment.

Bond funds used to be a safe haven for persons seeking high income, but this doesn't hold true any more. The fixed income market has experienced large swings in interest rates during the last few years, causing bond prices to fluctuate widely, along with the per share net asset values of the the mutual funds that invest in these securities. Bond prices move not only in response to the general level of interest rates, but also with inflation expectations and anticipated Federal Reserve Board policy. And the moves can be large. An illustration of this occurred when interest rates dropped in 1982 and 1985, and the prices of several bond funds gained more than 30%—something you'd expect from an aggressive growth fund.

Unfortunately, bond funds have also taken their lumps. Most long-term funds had very low total returns between 1977 and 1981, averaging between 1% and 5% a year. These poor results were caused by a trend toward higher interest rates. As rates went up, the value of the bonds in the portfolio decreased, offsetting the high yields from interest payments.

Some fund advisors employ a technique that is known as active fund management, whereby they trade debt securities in order to profit from interest rate changes or from disparities in value of different bonds. Their goal is to maximize returns over the short term, rather than hold bonds to maturity. However, any trading success may be partially negated by higher transaction costs.

Almost 50 high-yield or aggressive bond funds exist, and each has about 75 to 150 issues in its portfolio, providing excellent diversification for shareholders. The bonds average between 20 and 30 years to maturity, and have lower quality ratings in terms of the issuer's financial capacity to meet interest payments over an extended period of time.

Some high-yield bond funds are purchasing so-called "junk" bonds issued by companies in cyclical industries with low credit ratings and heavy debt burdens. These "B" or below rated bonds yield between 3% and 5% above the returns from "AAA," or the highest quality rated bond. And this yield spread usually widens during recessions and narrows in boom times because there is less risk of default. The idea behind high-yield bond funds is that through adequate diversification, risks can be spread among a variety of low-grade issuers. If one happens to default, it will have a small impact on total portfolio values. Meanwhile, junk bond fund investors are receiving premium yields for not that much additional total portfolio risk.

It's a good idea to stay away from any unit trust that invests in junk bonds. Unit trusts are similar to mutual funds, except the advisors purchase a fixed portfolio of bonds which are then held to maturity. However, the lack of active management of the holdings in these trusts is a major negative. The issuers of low-grade bonds must be constantly monitored regarding their often precarious financial condition. You don't want your fund to end up owning a bunch of deteriorating credit risks; when an issuer's credit quality starts to drop, the bond should be sold.

Another specialty fixed income fund on the investment scene is the Ginnie Mae fund. It provides a chance for the small investor, including IRA owners, to buy debt securities which offer higher interest rates (often a point or so better) than Treasury issues of the same maturity. They can be purchased in unit trust or mutual fund form. Ginnie Maes are a package of mortgages whose interest and principal payments flow through to the debt holders. If interest rates rise, then the principal payments slow because fewer people are refinancing their homes and paying off mortgages. Cash flows to Ginnie Mae holders also drop. On the other hand if rates drop, principal payments on the underlying mortgages will rise as more people refinance their home mortgages or pay them off when moving to another residence.

Ginnie Mae mortgage portfolios are U.S. Government-guaranteed. Ordinarily available only in $25,000 denominations, several mutual funds make the Ginnie Maes accessible to the IRA market for only a minimum investment of $1,000. Purchase of unit trusts can be made for as little as $250.

In addition to the longer-term fixed income funds, there are intermediate-term bond funds with average portfolio maturities ranging between five and ten years. Their values fluctuate less than long-term bond funds, but more than shorter-term funds. In the least risky category are found short-term bond funds and the well-known money market funds. The short-term funds usually invest in bonds and notes with maturities of less than a year. Although yields are higher than those of money market funds, there's a small loss of principal risk attached to owning short-term bond funds.

Money market funds, as everyone knows, are almost risk-free (there are even some funds that invest exclusively in government securities). Money market funds will normally be a part of every self-directed IRA portfolio. They should be used as a parking place for interest, dividends and other distributions pending reinvestment, or when you don't want to commit new funds to the stock or bond markets. All trustees or custodians of self-directed IRAs should automatically sweep idle cash into money market funds without any minimum investment requirement. Unfortunately, you're limited in your choice of money market funds to the one or two that a particular IRA trustee or custodian uses for its own account holders. You cannot comparison shop for higher rates.

Other Funds

For those persons with self-directed accounts that want some fast action in the stock market, an aggressive growth fund is probably the answer. In fact, it may be a good idea to place a small percentage of assets in one of these funds to provide another dimension to your IRA portfolio. But remember, you get no special benefit from capital gains in your IRA, and you can't deduct IRA losses from your adjusted gross income.

Aggressive growth funds are oriented toward maximum capital gains and may use special investing techniques, including leverage, to achieve these results. They are extremely volatile, performing very well in rising stock markets and very poorly in down markets. These funds are the best way for an investor to buy a portfolio of stocks that is likely to grow dramatically. Many better-managed growth funds have generated returns in excess of 20% annually during the past decade.

Aggressive growth funds should be held over the long term to maximize results. They most properly belong in the IRAs of younger persons who can time fund sales so they won't be forced to liquidate when the market is down. Aggressive growth funds are best bought when the stock market is making a strong upward move, which is when risk is lowest and reward greatest. Investing near the end of a market advance sharply changes the odds away from the investor's favor.

It should be pointed out that several mutual fund management companies have created special IRA funds. The sales pitch behind them is that the advisors are free to trade stocks as they see fit, because they won't be constrained to chose between taking short-term and long-term capital gains. They're not worried about the long-term capital gain period dictating when portfolio holdings should be sold. They can take advantage of short-term trading opportunities, moving to cash in response to market conditions, not as the tax man proscribes. IRAs are perfect for this strategy because earnings are tax-deferred and no distinction is made between short and long-term gains when taxes are eventually paid on distributions.

Many of these special IRA-oriented funds are relatively new. It's too early to assess their performance vis á vis other mutual funds. However, in the two years or so that they've been around, they haven't reached the top performer circle. Furthermore, the recent elimination of the tax preference for long-term capital gains will undoubtedly blur the distinction between the special IRA-type funds and other funds. In fact, of the five largest no-load special IRA funds in existence at the end of 1984, only one had more than a 115% portfolio turnover and three had less than 80%. This suggests that a lot less trading is taking place than was originally envisioned.

Choosing a Fund

Selecting the best mutual fund within the category of funds that is appropriate for your IRA is not an easy task. Many will have similar performance results and other characteristics. You can either consult with your financial advisor for funds that fit into your objectives, or you can try to pick them yourself.

The most obvious item to check before buying a mutual fund for your self-directed IRA is its past performance. Look at the record for a period of five to ten years or even longer. This will give a good reading on the fund's returns in both up and down markets. Make sure the results are not heavily skewed by one particular year when there was an unusually good or bad market. An example was the year 1974, when the stock market took a terrible beating. The performance results for most mutual funds were much better for the ten-year period 1975 through 1984, than for the period 1974 through 1985, because the former period excluded the disastrous results of 1974.

You should also check to see how long the current management has been with the fund. Maybe the good results were due to a hot-shot analyst who has since left for greener pastures. If you really want to conduct a sophisticated analysis of mutual funds, look at the risk-adjusted return (often described by the Greek word alpha) and the volatility of the fund over time (known as the fund's beta). This is particularly valuable information to have when selecting stock funds. Several services, including Computer Directions Advisors, Inc. and Lipper Analytical Services calculate these figures for mutual funds. Your broker or financial planner should be able to obtain this data for funds you're interested in buying.

Also be wary of large capitalization mutual funds—those with over $500 million in assets. The larger a fund, the harder it is for the manager to move in and out of individual securities without upsetting the market. In addition, the advisors of larger funds may have a more difficult time finding an adequate number of excellent investment opportunities, and the breadth of security ownership will dilute performance. Often a small fund establishes a superior track record and in response, many new investors join the shareholder ranks. The fund consequently becomes so big that its manuverability is constrained. It can't buy those low capitalization growth stocks that once used to make its portfolio perform so well.

One other admonition. Stay away from new funds, unless the managers have an established track record that is way above average. Often new funds try to capitalize on a stock market fad that's just about to burn out when the fund gets started. Mutual fund investors hop on the band wagon, only to be disappointed later with poor performance.

After the Fidelity fund group developed the special portfolio concept, industry-specific funds have come into vogue in the last several years. These funds buy into narrow sectors of the market, such as health care, utilities, financial services, telecommunications, energy and a host of other industries. Because they violate the principle of adequate diversification, they probably don't belong in IRA portfolios. However, some do very well in a year in which their particular industry has been a favorite of the stock market. But the industry funds at the top of the mutual fund performance derby today won't necessarily be there tomorrow. Stock market action rotates between groups and industries, and each has its day in the sun.

The oldest specialty funds concentrate in the precious metals industry and the international stock markets. A few have been around for years, and possibly could play an important role in some self-directed portfolios. The gold funds may offer a hedge against inflation, while the international funds provide a more broad geographical-based portfolio of stocks outside the United States.

Investing Techniques

Several investment techniques may be used with mutual funds. One is market timing. If you want to play this game, chose a family of funds or one with an arrangement with a money market fund which can accomodate telephone switching. If you like the market timing concept, but don't want to be bothered with anyalyzing technical data, you can employ a market timing service and pay them a management fee to move your money in and out of the market at the right moment. Or you can subscribe to a market timing newsletter.

Generally speaking, it's not a good idea to market time with mutual funds in your IRA. You have to be right twice—once when you're getting into the market and once when you are getting out. Because IRAs are for the long term, emphasis should not be placed on short-term fluctuations in the bond or stock markets.

Dollar cost averaging may be a more appropriate technique to use with mutual funds in your IRA. (It can also be done with individual stocks.) The objective is to lesson the risk of investing at the peak of the stock market. The idea is to invest a set amount of dollars in a mutual fund each month, regardless of whether the stock market is up or down. Strong discipline is the most important factor in maintaining a dollar cost averaging program—you musn't change your mind when the stock market begins to decline.

The investor hopes that eventually the price of the mutual fund shares will be higher than his average cost, because he was buying in both up and down markets. Some funds allow as little as $50 a month payments. If you're contemplating dollar cost averaging, then it is probably best to set up an IRA directly with the mutual fund IRA custodian. That way you'll avoid separate transaction charges on each purchase that some self-directed IRA trustees impose.

Dollar cost averaging can be done with an IRA where the $2,000 annual contribution is made early in the year. Put your lump sum contribution into the mutual fund's IRA money market fund on January 1st, and then instruct the fund or your self-directed trustee to make the stock mutual fund purchases at the beginning of each month or another appropriate interval. You're earning dividends from the money market fund while avoiding the market risk of investing all $2,000 at once. The chart below shows the effect of dollar cost averaging, assuming $500 is invested in a stock fund at the beginning of each quarter:

Date	*Net Asset Value of Fund*	*Number Shares Purchased*	*Cumulative No. shs.*	*Avg. Cost of All Shares*
1/1	$15.00	33.33	33.33	$15.00
4/1	14.00	35.71	69.04	14.48
7/1	14.50	34.48	103.52	14.49
10/1	15.50	32.26	135.78	14.73

At October 1, the average cost of the total 135.78 fund shares purchased was $14.73, which was $.77 below the net asset value of $15.50. The reason for this pleasant outcome is that during the second and third quarters, more shares were purchased at lower prices for the same $500.

This phenomenon of dollar averaging is another incentive to invest IRA monies in higher-yielding mutual funds. The cash distributions can be used to purchase funds on a periodic basis, thus hopefully lowering the average price paid if the market turns down. Another advantage is that, generally speaking, the higher the yield on a mutual fund, the more frequent the dividend payments. Thus, for high-yield bond funds and money market funds, payments are made monthly or quarterly. Your money is working faster for you as you reinvest those dividends. With growth funds, income dividends are usually paid out only once a year, at the same time capital gains distributions are made.

Closed-end Funds

Before leaving the subject of mutual funds, it should be pointed out that you can also buy shares in closed-end investment companies with your self-directed IRA. As the name implies, these funds only have a fixed number of shares outstanding. Open-ended funds, which represent the vast majority of mutual funds, issue new shares all the time at the day's net asset value per share (plus a sales charge in the case of load funds). Closed-end funds trade on a national stock exchange or in the over-the-counter market. Often they sell at prices below net asset value in down markets and close to net asset value in up markets. You pay a brokerage commission to buy one, but the fund managers do not charge shareholders for marketing costs to distribute shares, so their operating costs are generally lower.

The dual-purpose fund is an interesting type of closed-end fund for possible IRA investment. They were popular back in the late 1960s when several were formed. Dual-purpose fund shares are divided into two classes, a preferred stock (also referred to as an income share) that receives all the dividend income from the fund's portfolio, and a common stock (also referred to as a capital share) which is entitled to all of the capital gain when funds are liquidated at some future date.

The income shares are especially attractive for self-directed IRA investors because of their relatively high current yields and potential growth in those yields over time as the dividend income of the portfolio increases. The high yields make the share prices less volatile, but there's still potential for modest capital gains if the shares respond positively to higher dividends.

One other closed-end fund that should be seriously considered for self-directed accounts is the convertible fund. (There are also a few open-ended convertible funds.) These funds invest in a diversified group of convertible bonds and preferred stocks, and have the potential for generating relatively high current income and some capital appreciation. They're ideal for self-directed IRAs. The concept of the convertible security is more fully discussed in the section of this chapter which deals with stocks and bonds.

Limited Partnerships

Although limited partnerships are usually associated with tax shelters, many income-oriented ones make appropriate investments for IRAs. Very few of their tax benefits are wasted in the IRA. They provide good current returns with a chance for capital appreciation when partnership assets are sold. The sponsors of income-oriented partnerships avoid using leverage to purchase assets; most cash flows go to the limited partners rather than to service debt.

Limited partnerships consist of a general partner (often referred to as the sponsor or syndicator) who controls the business and financial activities of the partnership, and limited partners who are passive investors. This latter group puts up most of the capital, but also has limited liability with respect to the operation of the partnership. The general partner is the most important ingredient to the success of this type of investment. It should be financially strong with a solid net worth and be experienced in the business activities of the partnership.

The limited partners' share of the business's profit and loss flows directly to them; there's no intervening layer of tax at the partnership level. Partnerships invest in a variety of business activities, including real estate management, oil and gas production, equipment leasing, and cable TV systems. Partnerships can be purchased for IRAs only through a self-directed account.

Most income-oriented partnerships that would be logical IRA investments are registered with the Securities and Exchange Commission as public offerings. The sponsors set minimum investment amounts of $2,500, $5,000, or more for non-IRA investors, but lower these requirements to $2,000, or in some cases only $1,000, to accommodate the IRA market. The partnerships also have investor suitability requirements of $20,000 to $30,000 in net worth and gross income, or just $30,000 in net worth, not including automobile and home, but including the value of retirement accounts. These standards apply to all purchasers, including IRA owners.

Limited partnerships provide several benefits to self-directed IRA portfolios by offering attractive returns and a possible hedge against inflation. Their values are less volatile than stocks and don't have to be monitored every day, week or month, for they're meant to be held as long-term investments. Partnerships also offer a means of diversifying the IRA portfolio away from more traditional investments such as stocks, bonds and mutual funds. As an indication of how popular they've become with the IRA market, the sponsor of one income-oriented real estate program found two-thirds of its limited partners were IRA investors.

The major disadvantages of holding partnerships in IRAs are their lack of liquidity, the loss of some tax benefits, and the possibility of incurring unrelated business income taxes. Some financial advisors recommend against including partnerships investments in an IRA portfolio for just these reasons.

Partnership owners must look on their investments as a long-term commitment, which is consistent with the nature of IRA investing. Partnerships can last for as many as fifteen years before they're completely liquidated and the proceeds are paid to the limiteds. There is no exchange where partnership interests are actively traded (like stocks on the New York Stock Exchange), so you can't dump your investment in a hurry if you want to cash it in.

Obviously, persons nearing the mandatory IRA distribution age of 70 and 1/2 need to keep some of their IRA funds liquid to make enough withdrawals without having to pay the 50% penalty tax. A complete partnership interest may be transferred from the IRA to the owner, but this may result in a distribution greater than intended. IRA rules prohibit buying the partnership from the IRA for cash. Also, for those over 70 and 1/2, there's the annoying problem of valuing partnership interests each year in order to establish an IRA portfolio value to comply with IRS distribution requirements. To sum up, older persons should not load up their IRAs with limited partnerships.

There are ways to sell an interest in a limited partnership before it terminates, but the penalties could be severe. You will need to contact your broker or financial planner for assistance. Some general partners have buy-back provisions where each year a small number of limited partner's interests are repurchased. This is most prevalent with oil and gas income partnerships, but may also be found in some of the mortgage fund programs.

Several companies are in the market buying up "used" partnerships. These include Liquidity Fund of Emeryville, California and MacKensie Securities of San Francisco. A private outfit called the National Partnership Exchange (NAPEX) has also been established to facilitate trading in partnerships, but volume is low and it takes a while for a sell order to be matched with a purchaser. Trades are executed on the NAPEX through your broker who charges a commission for the sale.

Often the resale price of a limited partnership will be anywhere from 15 to 30% less than the liquidation value of the interest; the younger the partnership, the bigger the discount. Brokers and financial planners may also solicit other clients for interest in buying your partnership, but still expect to take a loss. The full benefits of partnership ownership are realized only when they're held to maturity.

IRA investors in limited partnerships also lose some tax benefits where depreciation and depletion are concerned. Even though the partnership may be unleveraged, part of the distributions to limited partners is usually treated as a return of capital and isn't subject to tax. This tax-sheltered cash flow is more valuable to a non-IRA holder. On the other hand, when the partnership is liquidated at a profit, no taxes are due if the limited partnership interest is held in an IRA. This can be an important benefit if recapture of prior depreciation benefits turns out to be a problem.

Finally, unrelated business income tax (UBIT) can affect certain IRA portfolios with a large portion of funds in partnerships. Congress legislated that pension funds, including IRAs, which invest in limited partnerships are actually owners of a business and subject to tax on their portion of the business's earnings. This prevents such tax-exempt organizations from using their special status to gain a competitve advantage over other businesses that must pay income taxes. UBIT is applied to the income from any trade or business that is not related to the tax-exempt purpose of a pension fund.

Fortunately, interest and royalty income, returns of capital, rents, and capital gains are not subject to UBIT. The first $1,000 of unrelated business income earned each year is not taxed. After that, the rate starts at 12% and moves up to a maximum of 50%. In the final analysis, UBIT should not be a problem for those who hold small amounts of partnership interests in their IRAs. In addition, losses from leveraged partnerships held by the IRA can be used to offset any unrelated business income.

Real Estate Partnerships

Several types of real estate limited partnerships make appropriate self-directed IRA investments. They can be purchased through brokers and financial planners or sometimes directly from the syndicator. The most popular for IRAs are unleveraged real estate equity programs, mortgage loan partnerships, and programs which combine the two. The characteristics of each are summarized below:

	Income	*Growth*	*Risk*
Unleveraged Real Estate	Med-low	Med-high	Med
Mortgage Loans	High	None	Med
Participating Mortgages	Med-high	Med-low	Med-high

No matter what type of real estate limited partnership you're considering, you should get a feel for the number and type of properties or mortgages to be purchased, their geographic location (national or regional), and whether they are to be constructed or existing properties. This analysis will provide additional information for assessing the various risks involved in making the investment.

Unleveraged public real estate partnerships take equity positions in a portfolio of apartment buildings, office buildings, shopping centers, business parks, warehouses, and even buildings housing fast food restaurants. A portfolio of properties is acquired in different geographical locations. Some syndicators specialize in a particular type of property, while others concentrate their purchases in one section of the country.

The general partner acquires properties for all cash or mostly cash and a small amount of debt. Unleveraged real estate partnerships offer IRA owners modest current yields along with capital appreciation potential. With little or no debt service, the risk of default is low compared to leveraged real estate investments. As long as occupancy rates remain high, rental increases will probably keep up with or outpace inflation. The properties should have a good chance of increasing in value, providing capital gains for IRA holders.

The actual investment results from an unleveraged real estate limited partnership depend on the expertise of the general partner, the income producing potential of the properties purchased, the fees and expenses charged by the general partner, and the profit split between the general and limited partners. In short, overall returns are often determined by the price paid for the property, the quality of the general partner management, and the correctness of timing of the property sale.

Naturally you should review the past performance of the general partner, paying particular importance to cash flows and returns on current partnerships, the results of prior partnerships, and sales of individual properties. These tables are found in prospectuses and offering materials but are often hard to interpret, so you may need the services of your investment advisor in this regard. A case in point: when figures such as average annual returns of prior partnerships are disclosed, have them converted to compound annual returns which is a more accurate measure of investment performance.

Mortgage loan partnerships have become popular because they offer relatively good current returns and the chance for a small amount of capital appreciation. You can chose from a wide variety of partnerships with different levels of yield and growth potential. Mortgage partnerships are of particular interest to IRA investors because they have lower risk than many corporate bonds offering comparable yields. The portfolio usually is made up of loans secured by investment-grade commercial property (a few partnerships invest in Federally-insured mortgages). However, investors have to look closely to see what percentage of loan-to-value ratio the general partner uses to approve loans—the greater the per cent, the riskier the loan.

The highest current yields are available in straight mortgage loan programs where the partnership doesn't participate in profits, cash flow or appreciation of the property. The partnership loans money on a property and receives a fixed rate of interest. Sometimes, part of the interest is deferred for several years until cash flows build up to a certain level or the property is sold. These latter programs may offer higher returns, but with the basic notion that a dollar today is worth more than a dollar received tommorow, the investor's overall risk is greater.

Any self-directed IRA investor concerned with inflation should consider purchasing participating mortgage loan partnerships. As the name suggests, the partnership not only receives current interest, but also a percentage participation of the increase in property rental income or appreciation. The property owner gives up some future value of the property in exchange for a lower interest rate on the loan. Either participating first or second mortgage loans can be made. The second mortgage is riskier and commands a higher rate of interest and greater participation in profits. In addition, the loan-to-value ratio is higher with a second, and it stands behind the first in the event of foreclosure.

Some mortgage loan syndicators make wraparound mortgages, commonly known as "wraps." These loans are wrapped around a smaller, existing first mortgage which usually has a low interest rate. Wraps facilitate financing for a purchaser who buys property with an assumable mortgage and needs to borrow additional funds to complete the deal. The wraparound lender services the underlying first mortgage and charges a higher overall rate, plus a participation in profits when the property is eventually sold. These wrap loans can be highly lucrative, but quite risky when a great amount of leverage is involved.

Many real estate syndicators have broadened their scope of operations to include mortgage lending. This is in response to the expanding, tax-deferred pension fund and IRA markets, which are attracted to high-yielding investments. The larger, more experienced syndicators should be well-equipped to manage partnership properties if the mortgages ever go into default.

As with unleveraged equity real estate partnerships, IRA investors should pay particular attention to promotional fees, management fees and the profit split between the general partner and the limited partners. Because very few syndicators have long track records in the mortgage loan business, it's diffcult to measure adequately their past performance.

Oil and Gas Income Partnerships

These income-oriented partnerships purchase existing oil and gas reserves, manage property operations, sell the hydrocarbon production, and then distribute the proceeds to limited partners. They usually do not drill new wells on the properties, but sometimes work over existing ones when production slows. Overall returns from these income partnerships depend on the price of oil and gas, the accuracy of the recoverable reserve count, and the amount of partnership reserves depleted each year.

Since the early 1980s, energy prices have declined, and with volatile prices the outlook remains uncertain. Expectations of future prices, however, are factored into the prices oil and gas syndicators pay for reserves at the time partnerships are formed.

Although oil and gas has provided a good hedge against inflation in the past, their prices haven't kept up with inflation recently, and there's no assurance they will in the future. Nevertheless, world energy reserves are dropping and oil and gas is another means of diversifying the self-directed IRA portfolio. And who knows, the oil and gas business may stage a comeback a few years from now.

The biggest drawback to using oil and gas partnership interests as an IRA investment is that their assets diminish over time as hydrocarbons are pumped out of the ground. Investor cash flows are partly a return of capital. This is an important concept to understand. The underlying value of the investment usually drops as the program extends out to its ten to fifteen year life. Therefore, it's unusual to reap capital gain income on oil and gas investments.

The value of oil and gas income programs can increase if more reserve quantities are recovered than was initially projected or if prices increase. The greater the uncertainty of future prices or actual reserves, the less the general partner will pay for new producing properties. Properties are bought on a discounted cash flow basis to establish a fair market price for reserves. The general partner's expertise in evaluating, selecting, and pricing acquisitions will be a key factor in the success of the investment. During periods of weak oil and gas prices, some general partners will locate distress sales of reserves. If the properties are efficiently managed, in the long run they'll generate good yields for the limited partners.

Investor returns from income funds also depend on the front-end costs of buying into the partnership (sales and property acquisition fees), management fees during the life of the partnership, and the cost and revenue-sharing arrangement between the general and limited partners.

It should be pointed out that some oil and gas income funds ran into trouble by borrowing to purchase reserves when the oil boom peaked in the early 1980s. When the price of oil dropped and reserve estimates proved to be over-optimistic, they experienced a severe cash flow crunch. The problems of Petro-Lewis and others are well-known to many of their investors.

As with most limited partnerships, oil and gas programs are not liquid. They must be held a long time, often up to fifteen years or more. This is greater than the life of a typical real estate partnership. However, some sponsors offer their limited partners annual presentment rights, whereby they repurchase a small number of partnership interests each year at a slight discount to reserve value.

One tax benefit that is lost to IRA investors in oil and gas programs is the tax-free return of capital represented by the depletion allowance. A certain percentage of each distribution goes tax-free to non-IRA investors, but no advantage accrues to IRA owners because they're already in a tax-free situation. However, oil and gas does provide another avenue of diversification for self-directed IRAs, and it can serve as an inflation hedge if oil and gas prices ever resume their upward climb.

Equipment Leasing Partnerships

Unleveraged equipment leasing programs are also potential IRA investments. Although the tax advantage from depreciation is lost, these programs can offer excellent cash flows and a quick return of capital, especially if lease rates are high compared to equipment costs. Equipment leasing partnerships offer one more opportunity for diversification of IRA portfolios away from the more traditional investments.

Equipment leasing programs are set up so that the general partner purchases equipment for the partnership and leases it for a period of months or years. Cash flows generated by the lease payments are paid out to the limited partners; however, as is the case with oil and gas programs, a portion of this represents a return of capital. Some equipment leasing programs lease equipment that is subject to fast obselescence. These must command higher lease rates to offset higher risks of re-leasing and lower residual values.

Total returns from equipment leasing should be higher that those available from corporate bonds. However, a lot depends on the residual value of the equipment after the leasing periods are up and the equipment is sold. Airplanes, peripheral computer equipment, and cargo containers have historically had high resale values, whereas mainframe computers haven't done as well. Like other partnerships, the investments are illiquid, but with equipment leasing the cash flows come early and the average holding period is usually a medium term of five to eight years.

Cable TV Partnerships

Cable TV limited partnerships have become popular of late because of the tremendous growth potential of the industry. They provide self-directed IRA owners an opportunity for capital appreciation and added diversification for the portfolio. Cable lends itself to the partnership form of business because of its high cash flows. Systems in the more rural areas of the country, where television is the major source of entertainment, have done quite well over the years. Construction costs are lower than in the big cities. Because cable TV is the "only game in town," the turnover rate for subscribers is low. Plus the recent cable deregulation bill gives system owners greater latitude in raising rates without regulatory approval.

The general partner buys cable systems and hopes to increase cash flows through better management of the systems. This includes increasing the number of subscribers through more intensive marketing, adding channels and premium services such as Home Box Office and Disney, building the system to outlying areas not serviced, and raising rates. The higher the cash flow, the greater the sales price when the system is eventually sold.

Cable TV partnerships are either income-oriented or use moderate leverage. Obviously, the former provides more immediate cash flow benefits to IRA investors; with the latter, the large tax benefits from depreciation are lost, but the magnitude of capital gain should be larger. Actually, because depreciation deductions are eventually recaptured as income when the systems are sold (similar to equipment leasing), total returns from cable programs are tax insensitive—they're about the same for both IRA and non-IRA investors.

Stocks and Other Equity-Related Securities

Certain common stocks are excellent investments for the larger self-directed IRA. They should be chosen with a view toward providing medium to high current returns with prospects for a small measure of dividend growth and capital appreciation over the longer term. Using the investment philosophy that a "dollar today is worth more than a dollar tomorrow," IRA investors should be willing to sacrifice the uncertainties of future price appreciation for high current yields and a chance for moderate growth.

What's the definition of a "high-yield stock?" It's all relative to the rest of the yields in the stock market, as measured by the Standard and Poor's 500 Stock Index or another market average. A yield of three to five percentage points above the market would probably be considered high-yield. For example, if the average market yield was 4%, then any stock with a dividend yield of 7% to 9% would meet the definition. As the stock market advances in a bull market, the level of yields tends to drop; as it declines in a bear market, the yield level rises.

You should plan on holding any common stocks in your self-directed IRA for a while. A study by the Hulbert Financial Digest, which tracks the performance of stock advisory newsletters, found that during a five-year period, only one newsletter that recommended trading outperformed those that had a buy and hold strategy—and that occurred in just one of those five years. Unfortunately, adhering to this investment strategy is easier said than done.

In some cases, you might be able to achieve your IRAs equity investment objectives by purchasing shares in a mutual fund. As explained previously, this may make sense if you're interested in going the aggressive growth route and don't want to manage a high-risk group of stocks on a daily basis. But only some IRA investors should be trying this approach—others need to follow a more conservative path.

Nevertheless, only a few mutual funds invest exclusively in a mix of high-yielding securities, including convertible bonds and preferred stocks, or write options to generate extra income. Here's where the self-directed IRA shines. You have the flexibility to invest in almost anything and can tailor your IRA portfolio to your own specific needs.

The principal drawback with purchasing individual stocks for an IRA is that the IRA can't be properly diversified when total funds in your account are small. If your IRA holds equal dollar amounts of only three stocks, and one of them drops in half, your portfolio will suffer a 16.7% loss. Even with five stocks, the loss is 10%.

The chart below shows what happens as you add stocks to your IRA holdings. The more stocks you have, the less total risk in the portfolio. This assumes that equal amounts of each security are purchased and no two stocks are of companies in the same industry. After you own six stocks, the risk reduction caused by adding more stocks diminishes from 5% to 2%; after ten stocks, marginal returns diminish even further.

Normally, you'll need at least ten stocks of companies in different industries to have an adequate amount of diversification–fifteen would be ideal. At first blush, this suggests at least a $20,000 to $25,000 self-directed IRA before you consider purchasing individual stocks. Of course, if husband and wife have IRAs, then the values of both accounts should be lumped together when considering whether to purchase common stocks.

However, because the self-directed IRA should be invested in medium to relatively high-yielding securities, the number of stocks in the portfolio could easily be less than ten. The rationale is that, as a rule, the stocks of high dividend payers aren't as volatile as other stocks.

Number of Issues in Portfolio	Percent of Total Risk	Percent by Which Risk Reduced	Cumulative Risk Reduction
1	100%	0	0
2	80	20	20
3	75	5	25
4	70	5	30
5	65	5	35
6	60	5	40
7	58	2	42
8	56	2	44
9	54	2	46
10	52	2	48
15	47	5	53
20	45	2	55

Their "betas" are low. (This term is used to describe how the prices of securities move in relation to the rest of the stock market.) The diversification offered by a low beta portfolio of five stocks cannot be matched by a high beta group of stocks containing as many as 25 securities. Also, the dividend of a high-yielding stock provides some downside protection against a drop in price.

You should pick yield-oriented stocks on the belief that their dividends are secure and will increase in the future. There are several ways to analyze stocks for these characteristics. You want to look at how often the company has raised its dividend in the past and what its current payment ratio is—the percent of earnings paid out to shareholders as common dividends. Has this changed in recent years? Also, ask yourself how certain the dividend is. Is it adequately covered by earnings and cash flow and what is the trend in coverage? For many stocks, there's a reason dividend yields are so high. You have to know why before you buy. Your financial advisor can help you with this analysis.

The utility companies are a good example of high-yielding stocks. Many have excellent dividends and are expected to increase them as their construction programs wind down. Some utilities are attempting to diversify into non-regualted areas to generate additional growth potential for their shareholders. Utilities involved in nuclear construction programs pay extemely high dividends, but the increased risk is probably not worth the extra current return for an IRA whose goal is preservation of capital.

The telephone companies are another group that pay relatively high dividends. Since the breakup of Ma Bell, there's been a competitive scramble for new business. Not only are the stocks of the Baby Bell companies available for purchase, but several regional telephone companies and independents also have good growth potential, both in the telephone busines and other areas of the telecommunications industry.

Bank stocks are also relatively high dividend payers. And future earnings growth will come from interstate banking as large banks buy up smaller regional ones. Many big-city banks are faced with problem loans, both domestic and foreign, but some of the regional banks have managed to put together solid growth records and their cash dividend payments have had a good upward trend.

A more general category for investment consideration includes blue-chip stocks which pay modest to high dividends and have some growth potential. Here one must proceed with more caution, as these stocks tend to be a trifle more volatile than those of utility and telephone companies. But total returns could be healthy if the right blue-chips are picked. One study shows that the best returns were garnered by selecting the ten stocks in the Dow-Jones average with the lowest price-earnings ratio at the beginning of each year and holding them for the full year.

As part of this "cheap stock" investment philosophy, you might want to take a contrarian view. Some of the most successful money managers have done very well for their clients by following this approach, which simply requires buying whenever everyone is selling and selling when everyone is buying. Contrarians like to profit from the crowd's mistakes. However, it takes discipline and patience, and above all courage to be successful with this stock selection technique. Self-directed IRAs are a natural vehicle to use, because contrarian investments should be made for the long term employing a buy and hold philosophy.

Contrarians look for well-managed, solid companies that are being ignored or are misunderstood by investors. They feel that over time, these unpopular and undervalued stocks will gain recognition for their fundamental worth and will rise in value. For example, back in 1982 the Pepsi-Cola Company (Pepsico) encountered problems on two fronts. The subsidiary in Mexico was floundering because of the constant devaluation of the Mexican peso. In addition, several executives were under the gun because of bribes to foreign governments. The stock was pushed down to below $35 a share. Several years later, when earnings were again on the upswing and these problems were long forgotten, Pepsico's stock was soaring to over $100 a share. And all the while, it was returning patient investors a 5% dividend yield based on the lower purchase price.

Another area of interest for self-directed IRA owners might be real estate investment trusts (REITs). These are like real estate limited partnerships in that they buy and manage properties or make mortgage loans and distribute earnings to shareholders. If most of income is paid out, then there are no income taxes due at the trust level. The big advantage REITs have over real estate partnerships is liquidity—their shares (also known as shares of beneficial interest) can be bought and sold just like any other publicly-traded stock. This feature makes them particularly suitable for older IRA holders who want the exposure to real estate, but are reluctant to sacrifice liquidity.

REITs pay out good dividends which often increase as the trust's advisors raise rents on the real estate holdings. The trusts also provide a hedge against inflation as long as the supply and demand for rental units remains in balance. As with the real estate limited partnerships, some REITS specialize in certain types of properties or in one or more geographical areas. Property holdings should be reviewed to gain a flavor for the makeup of the portfolio.

The finite real estate investment trust (FREIT) has become popular in recent years. Unlike the perpetual trust, the managers of the finite trust will sell off properties and liquidate it in five to ten years. FREITs were designed to overcome the stock market's reluctance to fully value the properties in a REIT portfolio. The stocks in the latter group often sell at a discount to actual market value of the real estate holdings. With a FREIT, these values hopefully will be realized by shareholders when the properties are liquidated.

Convertible bonds are a hybrid between a stock and a bond, but most persons classify them as a type of equity because their price movements are often tied to actions of the underlying common stock. Converts are becoming increasingly popular as pension fund investments. They're also a natural for larger self-directed IRA portfolios. They have downside protection thanks to the coupon rate of interest.

The lowest a convertible can sell for is as a straight bond based on yield. And they have upside potential to rise in concert with the price of the issuer's stock because of the conversion feature.

Convertible bonds appear to offer the best of both worlds. However, the investor pays for these benefits. The coupon rate of a convert will be lower than that of a comparable straight bond or debenture, and the conversion price will be set at a premium to the price of the underlying common stock. Most new convertible issues are sold at 15-25% premiums over the share price, and coupon rates of 2-4% less than a straight bond. Convertibles are no longer issued by marginal companies hoping to raise funds at a cheap rate; even Big Blue, IBM, has a convertible bond outstanding, the 7 and 7/8% due in the year 2004.

IRA investors shouldn't be led into a false sense of security by the investment value of a convertible bond, which is an estimate of how the bond would sell as a straight bond minus the conversion feature. The floor on the price of the bond can change over time, as interest rates go up and down. Furthermore, the investment value depends on the quality of the issue—bonds of high-quality issuers provide a much more stable floor than low-graded issuers.

Several rules of thumb should be followed when buying converts for your self-directed IRA. Don't buy one unless it sells for less than a 15% premium over the conversion value and less than a 50% premium over par value ($1,000). In order to figure the premium over conversion, use the following formula, where conversion value equals the market price of the underlying stock times the number of shares the bond is convertible into:

$$\text{Premium} = \frac{\text{Price of bond} - \text{Conversion value}}{\text{Conversion value}}$$

For a bond that is convertible into 50 shares of common stock and sells at $1,150 when the stock is selling at $20 a share, the premium is:

$$\frac{\$1{,}150 - \$1{,}000}{\$1{,}150} = \frac{\$150}{\$1{,}150} = 13.04\%$$

Another way to look at convertibles is to calculate how many years it takes to get back the premium from the extra yield of the convertible over the common. In other words, if the common is yielding 3% and the convertible is yielding 9%, the difference in yield is 6%. If the premium is 15%, then it will take 2.5 years before the difference is made up. The shorter the time frame, the more reasonably priced the convertible. Generally speaking, the premium should be recaptured through higher yields in three years or less.

Convertibles are sold in denominations of $1,000. Almost 300 of them are listed on the New York Stock Exchange. Another 100 or so trade on the American Stock Exchange. With a fairly active convertible bond market, self-directed IRA investors shouldn't be too worried about the spread between bid and asked prices.

There's one additional item to watch out for when purchasing convertibles. Check to see when the issuing company can force conversion. If this happens right after you've paid a stiff premium over conversion price, you could lose capital because all the company offers is either a small premium above par if you redeem, or the number of shares called for by the conversion terms. If a convertible is selling way above par, then there's a good chance the company will convert it in order to add more equity and clean up its balance sheet.

Although the above discussion dealt with convertible bonds, a related type of investment, the convertible preferred stock, shouldn't go without mention as an excellent purchase for self-directed IRAs. One investor statistical service follows over 200 convertible preferred stocks, so there's quite a variety to chose from. Many preferreds came into existence at the time of a merger, where a tax-free exchange of convertble preferred for common stock occurred and the higher dividend on the preferred was an inducement to get the shareholders of the acquired company to complete the merger.

Because they are equity securities, convertible preferreds are not as secure as convertible bonds. Interest on corporate debt must be paid ahead of preferred dividends. Also, there's no maturity date on the preferreds as is the case with bonds. Some preferreds may have sinking funds, whereby so many shares are retired each year. Dividends on convertible preferreds are paid four times a year, as opposed to the semi-annual interest payments of the bonds. This feature offers a faster compounding of returns in your tax-deferred IRA. In addition, you don't need a minimum of $1,000 to purchase convertible shares, as they usually trade in a range of $10 to $50 a share, and you can buy as few as you want.

Other types of equity securities may also be particularly suitable for IRA investors. The Americus Trust stocks are an example. The advisors take the stock of a large capitalization company and split it into separate income and capital gains components through the formation of a trust. These trusts are similar to dual-purpose funds discussed earlier in this chapter.

One set of trust holders receives all dividends plus a small portion of capital gains, while the other group receives all portfolio appreciation above a certain level. The income components are ideal for IRA investors, because they receive higher dividends than the underlying stocks pay, and they have a chance at a limited amount of capital gain. The AT&T Americus Trust was the first to be formed several years ago when Ma Bell was broken up; others are on the way.

Another interesting security may appeal to IRA investors who don't want to get locked into oil and gas income funds of the limited partnership variety. This is the master limited partnership (MLP), which has not only the liquidity of a common stock, but also a high yield. Master limited partnerships are usually formed by oil companies who either consolidate or roll up existing income or drilling partnerships, or through a reorganization, roll out their own production fields. The new ownership interests are represented by depositary receipts or units which are listed on one of the national exchanges or traded in the OTC markets.

Unlike income partnerships, many MLPs retain some cash flow to finance more drilling on existing properties. Large MLPs are not as risky as the income partnerships because they have a more diversified base of oil and gas properties. However, as with limited partnerships, you lose income tax benefits, such as the depletion allowance and the intangible drilling expense that you'ld be entitled to if the investment was held outside the IRA.

Several techniques are available for self-directed IRA investors to increase returns from a portfolio of equity securities. You can participate in the company's dividend reinvestment or stock purchase plan as long as the stock is held in the name of the trustee or custodian for the benefit of you, the IRA owner. Street name only holders (i.e., the name of your stock is held on your behalf in brokerage house name) can't join these special programs.

The advantage of the dividend plan is that you can use your dividends to buy additional shares in the company at a price slightly below market price or at the market at minimum commission cost. With the stock purchase plan, you can add to your dividends being reinvested and buy extra shares at a discount to market (usually 5%) from your own funds. There's a dollar cap on the amount of stock you can buy.

In effect, with a dividend reinvestment plan you're dollar cost averaging the price of the shares, particularly when you buy extra shares when the price of the stock is down. In order to implement this technique, shares are purchased throughout the year at quarterly intervals, regardless of how the stock market is doing. If you have a stock that's paying an 8% dividend, then you're buying an 2% additional shares each quarter.

The main disadvantage of using the dividend reinvestment technique is that you're not building up cash in your self-directed IRA to take advantage of other special investment opportunities when they arise. Also, with a smaller IRA, you should probably use the cash dividends to seek further diversification of your portfolio, rather than reinvest them in shares of the same company. Therefore, dividend reinvestment programs are best utilized by those persons with large self-directed accounts.

One other technique you can use to increase your IRA income is to write covered call options. This limits both risk and return but is popular with some pension fund managers. There's no reason IRA investors can't follow suit. It's the most conservative approach to playing the options market, and can be done with your self-directed IRA funds under current regulations.

The option writing technique is a way of raising your overall returns several percentage points. It is particularly attractive with high-yielding stocks, although the option premiums received are not large. However, if you aren't in a position to own stocks in your IRA, then you shouldn't go out of your way to buy them just to write options.

If you own a stock that has underlying calls traded on one of the options exchanges, you can write either a three, six, or nine-month call on it. You take in the call premium and still collect the dividends that are paid on the stock that you own. The call premium can amount to 3% to 4% of the price of the stock, so this is a nice bonus on top of the high dividend. The call or striking price may be below, at, or above the current price of the stock. Because you really don't want the call exercized and the stock sold out from your IRA portfolio, it's usually best to sell a call that's at a strike price a bit above the price of the common.

Your greatest risk is that the stock advances in price and is called away from you. In this case, you won't profit from any price appreciation above the call price. Another risk, of course, is that the price of the stock will decline. However, the call premium will offset part of the decline, and anyway you're usually not too concerned with short-term downward price movements of stocks in your self-directed IRA. Remember, you're supposed to be holding for the long term.

Here's how the call writing technique works. (No provision for commissions or other transaction costs is taken into account.) You own 100 shares of a stock which sells for $28 a share. You sell a six-month call for $2 or $200 at a strike price of $30 a share. The stock pays a $1.50 dividend for a 5.4% yield. If the price stays the same and the call expires unexercised, then you have a total return of $200 from the call and $75 from half a year of dividends. Your annual yield is 19.1%, all tax-free because it's in your IRA. If the stock goes up to $35 and the call is exercised, then your total return is $475 (add in the $200 profit), or 33.9% on an annualized basis. Of course, when this happens, you lose the opportunity for a $500 profit. If the price of the stock drops to $25, then your loss has been cushioned by the proceeds from the call, which will expire unexercized under this scenario.

Call premiums vary with the volatility of the underlying common stock. The greater the historical price fluctuations of the shares, the larger the premium as a percentage of the stock price. With stocks that are most suitable for IRAs, premiums will be relatively small because there's not as great a chance that the calls will be exercized. But this technique is still an excellent way to add extra income to your IRA holdings without taking on extra risk.

One final point. Because the cost of selling a single call (up to 10% of its price) and the underlying stock could eat up a lot of the profit in writing calls, it's usually best to write several at once. To do this you need several hundred shares of a particular stock, which means your IRA holdings must be relatively large before you employ this technique. Or you could negotiate lower commissions with your broker to keep transaction costs down.

You have been presented with a variety of investment options—more than you probably ever thought possible with an IRA, let alone a self-directed one. How you select these securities for your portfolio will depend on a number of factors. Even if you don't handle the IRA investment selection yourself, this information will put you in a better position to review the recommendations of your investment advisors. A little knowledge goes a long way, especially when it comes to investing your IRA dollars wisely. In the next chapter, you'll learn some portfolio allocation techniques which will help you determine how much of each type of security should be in your self-directed IRA.

CHAPTER 7

IRA Portfolio Allocation Techniques

After having established goals and objectives for your self-directed IRA, and having reviewed the various investment alternatives available, you must put together the appropriate portfolio that meets your needs. This includes deciding on the best mix of money market equivalents, stocks, bonds, and other investments. As explained below, several methods or combinations of methods may be used in the portfolio allocation process. You can either undertake this task yourself, or use the services of an investment advisor or financial planner.

This book will not recommend the ideal portfolio mix for your self-directed IRA, because each person's personal circumstances vary greatly and economic conditions are always changing. There's no correct answer for all persons for all time; what's right for one person may be wrong for another person or wrong for both at different points in time. However, Chapters 11 though 13 present case studies of various IRA owners, along with recommendations on how their portfolio mix might be improved to suit their preferences or particular circumstances. This will provide some guidance on how to use the self-directed IRA to maximum benefit.

Pension fund managers have the same problem of trying to develop appropriate portfolios to match the goals and objectives of the groups they work for—pension plan administrators and trustees. These professionals attempt to balance needs by dividing portfolios among short-term funds, equities, fixed-income securities, and other investments. However, because of the enormous size of most pension funds, the managers really don't have the flexiblity that smaller IRA investors enjoy in moving assets among a variety of investment alternatives.

According to a Pensions and Investment Age survey of the 200 largest pensions funds, their portfolios were invested as follows, at September 30, 1984:

Stocks	41 2%
Bonds	33.4
Money Market Equivalents	10.4
Real Estate	8.4
Guaranteed Income Contracts	3.0
Other	3.6
Total	100.0

This illustrates how conservative money managers of pension funds are in their fiduciary capacities of dealing with huge pensions that eventually will have to be paid out to thousands, even millions of separated and retired employees. Only a little over 40% is invested in the stock market, with about 47% going into fixed-income securities. Real estate is the fastest growing segment, now approaching 10% of assets in the average large pension portfolio.

Many of the same principles used by professional pension plan administrators can be applied by the IRA holder through the self-directed approach. Not surprisingly, the factors which influence the investment decisions of the former group are similar to those facing the IRA investor. The chart on page 105 depicts this phenomenon.

Pension managers and IRA holders also operate with numerous constraints placed on them, such as a fixed time horizon, the need for some liquidity, certain risk tolerance levels and minimum diversification requirements. These also have to be factored in when constructing a pension portfolio that eventually will be used for retirement income.

Various Techniques

The IRA portfolio allocation process can be approached in several ways. Some experts advocate shifting funds among money market instruments, stocks, and bonds as economic conditions change.

Factors	*Pension Fund*	*IRA Investor*
No taxes paid on current income and capital gain income	Yes	Yes
Restrictions on type of investments	None	Very few
Liquidity considerations	Some	Some
Incentive to maximize returns to reduce costs	Yes	No*

* The IRA holder wants to increase the value of his account, consistent with taking reasonable risks. This objective is actually similar to the goal of pension plan administrators, because both want relatively high rates of return with minimal risk.

When the economy is about to start on its upward path of the business cycle, the investor would be wise to shift emphasis out of bonds and into the stock market. These conditions should be bullish for stocks, but bearish for bonds as interest rates rise in a heated economy.

As the business cycle nears its peak, the IRA investor should move funds out of the stock market and into bonds. This is the time when inflation slows down and the Federal Reserve loosens credit. Stocks prices will usually decline and bonds will become more expensive as yields drop.

You can try your hand at guessing the peaks and troughs of the business cycle; however, this is often difficult to do with any consistency. It may be slightly easier to make a move once a clear trend has been underway for some time. Even the best economists have trouble trying to make accurate predictions of what the inflation rate will be over the next year, let alone the percentage by which gross national product will grow. Your task will be just as hard. This economic timing approach may or may not work for you. But in any event, expected changes in economic conditions should have an influence on the portflio mix you chose at any particular point in time.

A slightly different approach is used by professional stock market timers. They look at cash flows going into and out of the stock market to determine whether it will go up or down. They believe major turns are based on investor psychology. Net cash flows into the market are a bullish sign: net outflows are a bearish sign.

One advantage with doing timing in an IRA or with any other tax insensitive funds is that there's no concern over the tax consequences of short-term trading. Good market timers will switch out of stocks into money market equivalents on a moment's notice when either the bond or stock market is moving down. Most mutual funds, on the other hand, generally don't go heavier than 30% into cash positions. Some investors find there's too much constant exposure to the stock market with equity mutual funds—they're more comfortable with the pure timers.

The market timers like to chart how an investment would perform, both with and without the benefit of market timing. A picture of the results of a successful timer will no doubt end up looking like the graph on the right side:

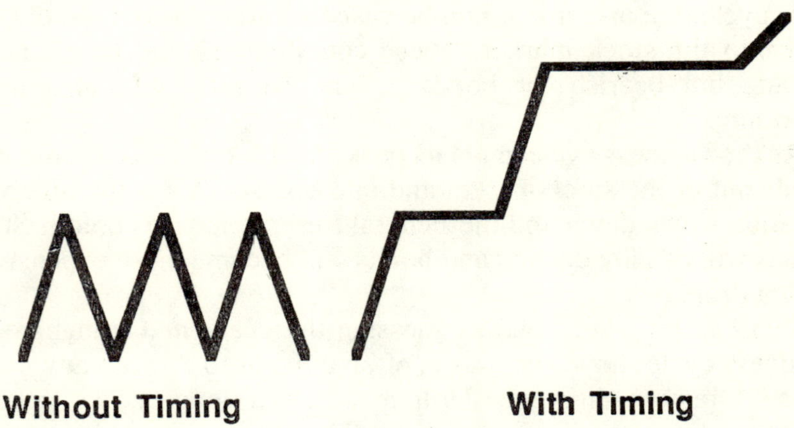

Market timers time with mutual funds (usually with the no-load variety), moving back and forth between aggressive growth funds and money market funds. (There's even a bond timing fund that shifts between bond mutual funds and money market funds.) Some have had good records in recent years, but the technique is too new to be fully tested over a long period.

Unfortunately, the minimum fees charged by most market timers are too steep for a small IRA. They can range upwards to 3% of net assets per year. If you have built up your account to more than $25,000, or had a large rollover, then it may be worthwhile to pay for the services of a timer. Also, some mutual funds practice timing as part of their investment strategy. There's no extra fee for this service and the cost to the small IRA investor is much less.

Another portfolio allocation technique is to divide up assets according to your beliefs about expected returns from each investment category. Again, the three basic types of assets—money market instruments, stocks, and bonds—are considered. Expected total returns (income and capital gain or loss) for each of the asset types are estimated and the amount of risk an IRA investor is willing to take is considered.

Predicting investment returns over the next few years can be a formidable task for the non-professional IRA investor, as well as the astute academics with their sophisticated computer models. Therefore, inflation rate expectations may be subsitituted as an indicator of how different types of investments will perform. With various rates in mind, estimates of expected returns and their variability can be made for short-term debt, stocks and bonds, as shown below:

Total Annual Returns At Expected Inflation Rates of:

	2%	4%	6%	8%
Money Market	6	7	10	12
Stocks	15	12	10	5
Bonds	10	8	7	3

An appropriate portfolio can be developed based on these inflation expectations. For example, an IRA investor looking for relatively high inflation rates of 10% would put a heavy percentage of assets into money market instruments, where the yields might reach 15%. On the other hand, someone forecasting lower inflation rates of 4% would be more inclined toward the purchase of stocks for an IRA, for this strategy would earn a total return of 12%.

Another portfolio allocation technique is to convert your personal IRA investment objectives into a portfolio mix which most closely reflects them. For example, objectives such as high current income, long-term growth, safety of principal, and low variability can be weighted or ranked in importance. A composite may be translated into various mixes of money market, stock and bond assets in the self-directed account. This is not a timing approach; it's directly keyed into your goals and objectives as they relate to risk and return. You change the mix, based on changes in your objectives.

For example, a typical IRA investor might set up the following table and assign weights to each of the goals, where a "1" is very important, a "3" is moderately important, and a "5" is not too important.

	Type of IRA Investor		
	Conservative	*Average*	*Aggressive*
High current income	1	3	5
Long-term growth	5	3	1
Safety of principal	1	3	5
Low variability	1	3	5

A score or 16 (three fives and a one for long-term growth) denotes an aggressive investor who would allocate all IRA funds to equities, presumably in aggressive growth stocks or mutual funds. On the other side of the coin, a person with a total score of 4 would tend to be very conservative and invest about half of his IRA funds in money market funds and the other half in medium-term bonds. Many IRA investors will fall somewhere between the two extremes, but on the low side of the 6 to 10 range with an emphasis on high current income and safety of principal, along with a moderate amount of capital gain. This might result in a portfolio weighted 40% in income-oriented stocks, 40% in bonds and 20% in money market funds.

Managing Portfolio Risk

No matter which portfolio allocation technique is chosen, you'll want to be sure your self-directed IRA is adequately diversified. The objective is to minimize risk, so that if one investment goes bad, the value of the whole IRA will not be affected in any significant way. All rational investors would like to preserve principal, have it readily available, and maximize total returns at the same time. Unfortunately, all these objectives can't be achieved simultaneously–tradeoffs have to be made.

Risk can be defined as the variability of an investment's expected rate of return. The greater the variation, the greater the risk. This is shown in the following chart, where each type of security (except money market instruments) has a different bell-shaped curve:

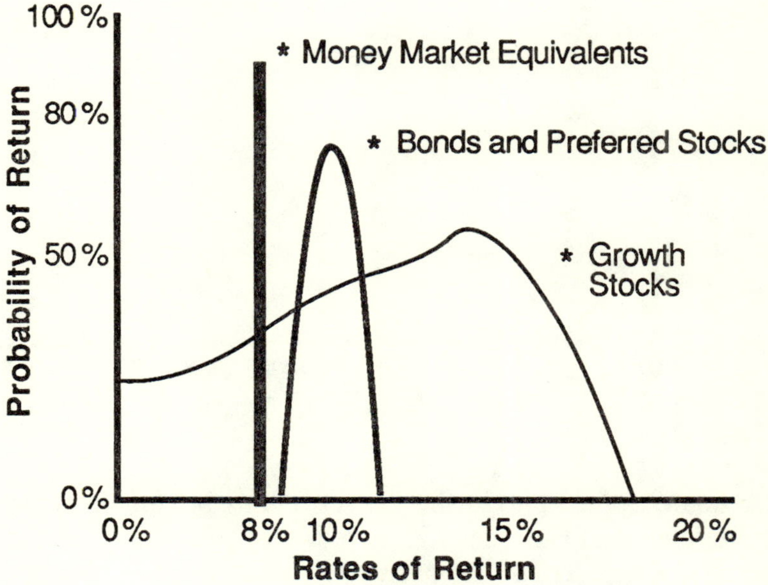

Money market instruments have the least amount of variability as far as rates of return are concerned, but also offer the lowest rates. Growth stocks, on the other hand, have the greatest potential rate of return, but with the most variability. Bonds fall somewhere in the middle of the other two securities.

The five specific types of risk associated with investing are purchasing power risk, interest rate risk, market risk, business risk, and industry risk. Sometimes the first and second risks are related, for interest rates often go up with inflation. If your IRA investment returns fail to keep pace with inflation, then you're an unfortunate victim of purchasing power risk. Fixed-income investments are most exposed to this type of risk, as they are with interest rate risk. You

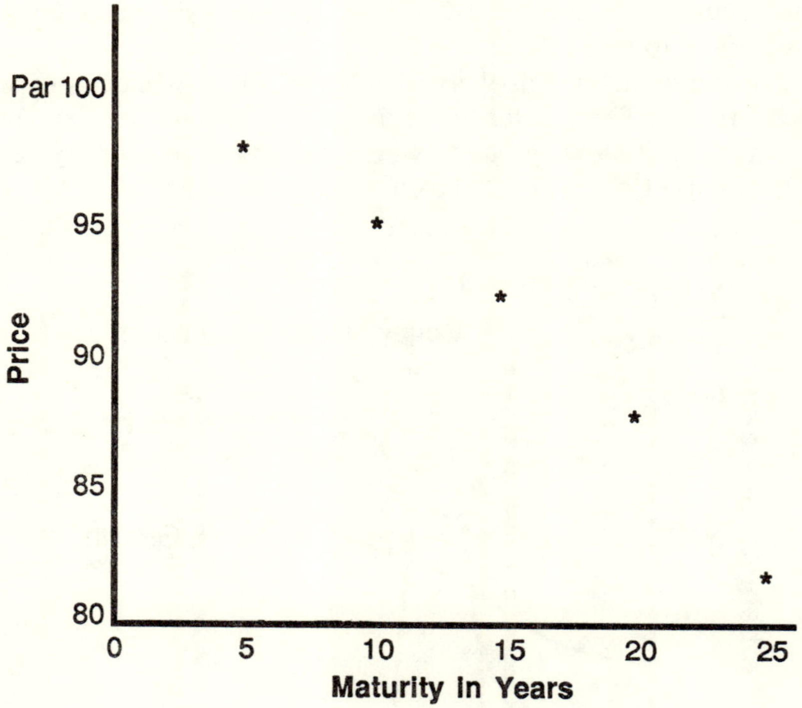

can insulate against purchasing power risk by holding investments in your self-directed IRA that will increase in value if inflation goes up. Historically, real estate has been cited as just such an investment.

Interest rate risk is the risk of loss of principal due to fluctuations in the level of interest rates. As interest rates move up, the prices of bonds move down to adjust to the higher current returns available in the market place. This risk is most prevalent in the medium and long-term bond market; as interest rates move up and down, the prices of these bonds fluctuate greatly.

The diagram above indicates this phenomenon. Assume five bonds with maturities ranging from 5 years to 25 years are each selling for par. If interest rates rise by two percentage points, the price of all the bonds will drop. Depending on the yield curve, longer maturities will drop in value more than shorter maturities. And the difference could be as much as 15%, just on a two point rise in interest rates.

The primary way to protect against interest rate risk is to hold short to medium-term securities. You especially don't want to hold long-term zero coupon bonds because they will lose value the quickest if rates go up.

Market or systematic risk is the risk that a general decrease in stock market prices will cause the prices of the securities in your IRA portfolio or mutual fund to go down, irrespective of their underlying fundamental value. When the broad market indicators go up and down, the prices of most stocks follow suit. Various studies have shown that one-half of the movement in individual stock prices is accounted for by market fluctuations.

One way to protect yourself against this type of risk is to buy stocks of companies traded in foreign stock markets, which often move in the opposite direction of the United States market. Another way is to buy stocks of gold and silver companies, whose shares often rise in price when the stock market declines.

Industry risk is the risk that a whole industry will experience financial difficulties and all companies in it face the same adverse outcome. This could be the result of increased foreign competition, changes in government policies or general economic conditions, or new technologies. Recent examples of industry risk have been the declines in the oil business, the steel industry, the nuclear power industry, the farm equipment industry, and the electronics business.

Industry risk can affect the values of both stocks and bonds in your self-directed IRA. Lower cash flows and earnings impact the ability of the company to declare dividends on their common stock and make interest payments on their debt. The best way to insulate your IRA portfolio against this risk is to diversify holdings across industry lines.

Business or unsystematic risk is the possibility of a failure or temporary set back for one particular company in which you have invested your IRA funds. Again stocks and bonds are both subject to this risk. The risk of financial collapse, even bankruptcy, can come from bad management practices, lack of adequate financing, or a combination of the two. Firms with high business risk will be characterized by flucutating sales and profits. They may be in cyclical industries, or they could be growth companies that stop growing. As with industry risk, the best way to deal with business risk is to diversify adequately.

Your total IRA portfolio risk is a function of the type of individual investments in it. Each security has some degree of independence from and interrelationship to other securities in the portfolio. This could be a positive or negative number; if positive, the security values move together. If negative, the values move in opposite directions. Likewise, some stocks have higher betas because their movements are greater than the market; others have low betas and move less than the market. A security with a beta of one moves in concert with the market.

If you want to minimize overall risk in your IRA portfolio, then you should select investments that move in opposite directions from one another. Therefore, when one sector decreases, the other will increase. According to modern portfolio theory, the impact of a particular security on the overall portfolio depends on its return, its risk (uncertainty of return) and the movement of it in relation to others, known as covarience. It's strange but true that the addition of a risky security may make the overall portfolio less risky than by adding a conservative security. On the other hand, if it's the same as the others, it does little to reduce total portfolio risk.

Some investments which have historically moved in opposite directions from one another are paired below:

Bonds–real estate
Yield stocks–growth stocks
Gold and silver–stocks
U.S. stocks–international stocks
Money market yields–stocks
Capital goods stocks–defensive stocks
Oil stocks–airline stocks

Those whose prices tend to move together include:

Stocks–bonds
Yield stocks–bonds
Bank stocks–bonds
Building stocks–bonds

There's another trap to avoid with your self-directed IRA: don't overload it in one direction. For example, if you think interest rates are going to drop, invest in interest-sensitive stocks, but don't lengthen your bond portfolio at the same time by switching from short-term to long-term bonds. This gives you a double risk exposure. If you're wrong and interest rates rise, you'll be hurt twice. In this situation, you should probably hedge your IRA portfolio by staying short in the bond market.

Portfolio Liquidity

Another point to keep in mind when considering the proper portfolio mix for your self-directed IRA is your need for liquidity. Absolute liquidity is the ability to sell an investment and raise cash quickly without losing principal or forfeiting interest. You might have several reasons for wanting to liquidate part of your portfolio in a hurry. You may want to take advantage of an unusual investment opportunity. You may need to make an emergency withdrawal. You may want to begin periodic withdrawals at age 59 and 1/2, or you must begin mandatory distributions at age 70 and 1/2. Whatever the reason, it's nice to have some ready cash or cash-equivalents in your self-directed IRA at all times.

The following categories of IRA-type investments are ranked according to liquidity, with the most liquid appearing first;

Very Liquid	1. Cash
	2. Money market funds
	3. Short-term bonds
Moderately Liquid	4. Medium-term bonds
	5. Stock and bond mutual funds
	6. Stocks
	7. Long-term bonds
Illiquid	8. Limited partnerships

The percentage of your IRA portfolio kept very liquid may vary from 5% to 20%, or even higher if you're practicing market timing techniques. If the IRA is your only source of potential cash for an emergency fund, then you'll probably want to hold a higher percent in liquid securities.

Historical Rates of Return

At this point in the discussion of portfolio allocation techniques, it would be worthwhile taking a look at the historical rates of return provided by various types of investments. Fortunately, one such study has been conducted by Goldman Sachs and Company, the New York investment banking concern. It compares returns for common

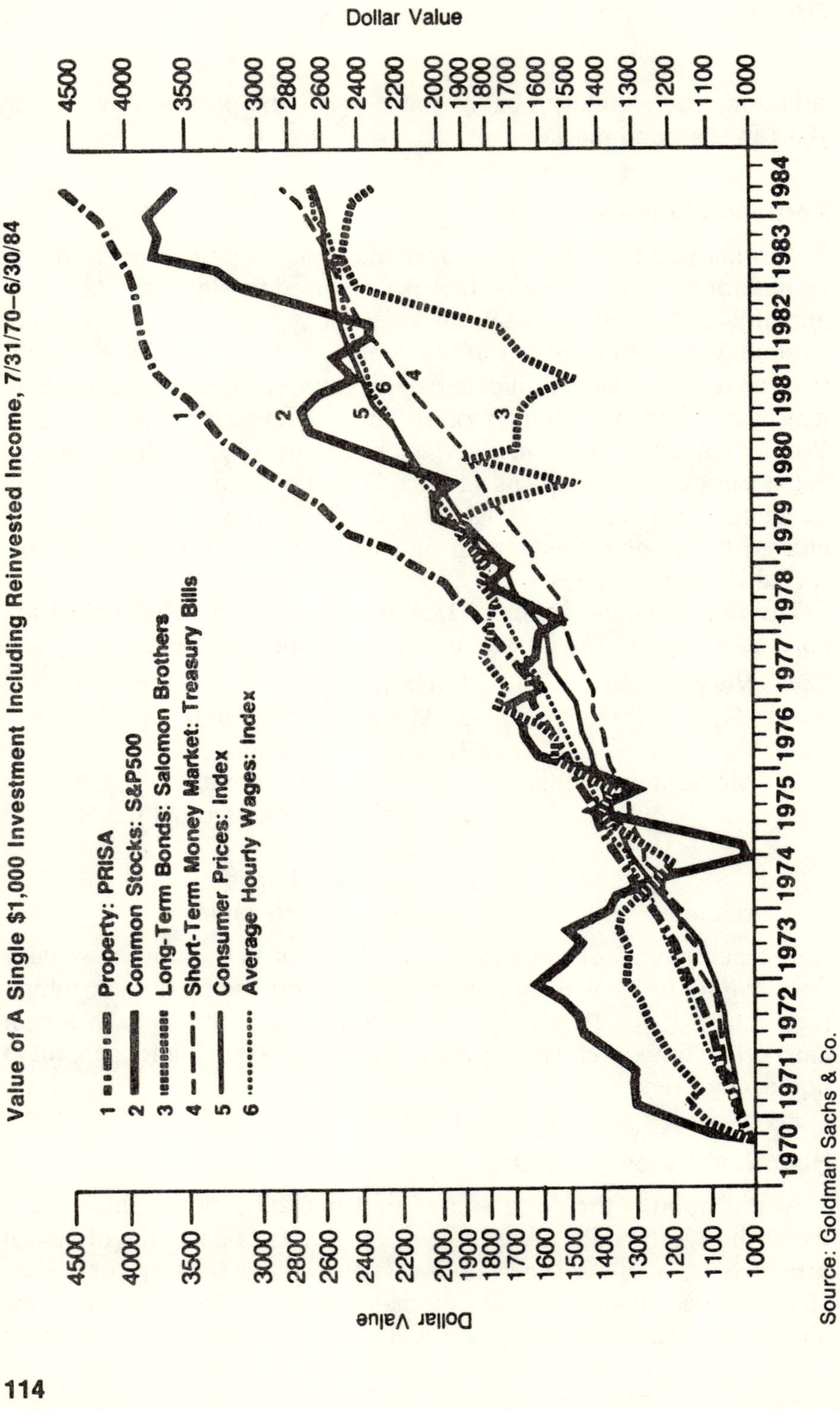
Value of A Single $1,000 Investment Including Reinvested Income, 7/31/70–6/30/84
1 Property: PRISA
2 Common Stocks: S&P500
3 Long-Term Bonds: Salomon Brothers
4 Short-Term Money Market: Treasury Bills
5 Consumer Prices: Index
6 Average Hourly Wages: Index
Dollar Value
4500
4000
3500
3000
2800
2600
2400
2200
2000
1900
1800
1700
1600
1500
1400
1300
1200
1100
1000
1970
1971
1972
1973
1974
1975
1976
1977
1978
1979
1980
1981
1982
1983
1984
Source: Goldman Sachs & Co.

stocks, long-term bonds, short-term money market instruments, and real estate with the consumer price index and average hourly wages. The chart, reprinted on page 114, shows how the value of a $1,000 investment, including reinvested income, has fared during the period from July 31, 1970 to June 30, 1984.

Although fourteen years is not a relatively long period of time, it does indicate the most recent performance figures. The reason the performance does not go back further in time is that the real estate figures are only available for that period. The Prudential Insurance Company of America created its Prudential Property Investment Separate Account (better known in the financial and real estate communities as PRISA) in July, 1980. This open-ended, commingled account has gross assets of over $4 billion held collectively for over 400 pension funds. It's the world's largest pooled pension real estate fund and has the longest operating history of any major property fund in the United States.

The table below shows the compounded rates of return, both in nominal dollars and in real dollars (adjusted for inflation):

Value of $1,000 Investment in Selected Vehicles, 7/31/70–6/30/84

	Nominal Dollars		*Real Dollars*	
	Amount	*Annual Return*	*Amount*	*Annual Return*
Property–PRISA	$4,582	11.6%	$1,742	4.1%
Common stocks–S&P 500	3,583	9.6	1,362	2.2
Long-term bonds–Salomon Bros. Index	2,348	6.2	892	(0.9)
Short-term investments–90-day T-bills	2,845	7.8	813	0.6
Average Hourly Wage Index	2,644	7.2	1,005	0.0
Consumer Price Index	2,631	7.2	1,000	0.0

Not surprisingly, real estate fared best during this time, with a compound growth rate of 11.6%. The high inflation rate of the 1970s certainly helped its performance. Stocks did next best with a 9.6% return, thanks mainly to a stellar performance since August, 1982. This is slightly above the longer-term historical rate of 9% for stocks. Long-term bonds ended up in last place because of the general rise in interest rates during the 1970s. This loss of capital offset the high current yields available in many of those years. It should also be noted that these returns were calculated from starting points which were near the June, 1970 bottoms for both stocks and bonds.

It goes without saying that history rarely repeats itself, especially when the financial markets are concerned. There's no assurance that real estate will continue to outperform the other types of investments, or that stocks will repeat their above-average performance. No one can predict for sure what investments will do best in the future. That's why a diversified self-directed IRA portfolio is a must. The role of each of the major categories of investments will be examined next.

Role of Money Market Instruments in IRA Portfolios

Money market equivalents have a prominent role in the management of a self-directed IRA. This is where funds should be parked in times of uncertainty, particularly when an investor is concerned that the stock or bond markets are too high. This type of investment will be particularly important to those who try to time market movements.

Money market funds have no risk of principal loss, although their yields will vary with the general level of short-term rates. Considered the safest and most secure of all investments, their total returns will usually be modest. Most self-directed IRA investors will always have some portion of their funds in the money market, even if it's only interest and dividend payments that were swept in from other investments, waiting to be reinvested at the right moment.

Role of Fixed-Income Securities in IRA Portfolios

Among the most popular types of IRA investments, particularly zero coupon bonds, fixed-income securities are in the middle when it comes to risk and return, even though the Goldman Sachs' statistics indicate they've had a rocky road of late. Bonds have a promised stream of cash flow consisting of interest payments and a date certain when the principal is to be paid. This is supposed to give the investor greater confidence in these securities. In recent years, there has been an increasing volatility associated with the fixed-income markets, particularly the one for long-term bonds, as interest rates have fluctuated widely within relatively short periods of time.

Fixed-income securities should probably represent a smaller percentage of the total IRA portfolio for young persons, and a higher percentage for older persons. For those needing liquidity, short-term securities are best, even though an IRA portfolio may sacrifice several percentage points in yield. The maturities may also be staggered (using zero coupon bonds) to provide steady cash flows.

Persons with self-directed accounts should not try to trade bonds. Most fixed-income investments for IRAs will probably be purchased through the mutual fund medium to gain maximum liquidity and diversification for a small amount of funds. You should let the professional bond analysts move up and down the yield curve searching for the best values, rather than attempt this yourself.

Role of Equities in the IRA Portfolio

Equities are more volatile than fixed-income securities and should be held for the long term. The common stock does not promise anything, but has the potential for high returns through growth in corporate earnings and dividends. Exposure to the stock market entails the greatest risk, although this can be minimized somewhat by investing in higher-yielding, less volatile stocks.

The high-yield investment manager will look for undervalued stocks with high current dividends, low price-earnings ratios, and a low market to book value ratio. You or your advisor should do the same when searching for individual stocks for your self-directed IRA portfolio. Or you should find a mutual fund manager with the same philosophy of equity investing.

The weighting of equities in your portfolio should be consistent with your IRA objectives. Although capital appreciation is usually the byword of equity investing, this is not necessarily true for IRA owners who want to emphasize current income. A person approaching retirement age should think about selling stocks in his self-directed IRA approximately five years ahead of time, for he certainly doesn't want to be bailing out in a down stock market when liquidity is needed.

Over the years, common stocks have shown good growth rates. Recently, the equity markets have performed extremely well. With a proper selection of individual stocks, convertible bonds, or mutual funds that invest in these securities, this part of your self-directed

IRA portfolio should do quite well as long as the American economy maintains its overall historical growth patterns. And it helps even more if you and your professional advisors can beat the market averages.

Role of Real Estate in IRA Portfolios

Many pension funds have begun to increase the exposure of their portfolios to real estate. A study by Greenwich Research Associates showed that between 1979 and 1983, the percentage of Fortune 100 companies with real estate in their pension plan portfolios increased from 30% to 74%. This investment medium has provided attractive total returns from both current income and capital appreciation.

In periods of unexpected high inflation, when real returns on stocks and bonds diminish, and in some instances become negative, real estate has generated positive returns. Real estate values are less likely to drop in uncertain periods, although the rate of appreciation varies from time to time. Currently, with lower inflation rates and oversupplies of rental properties in some markets, real estate returns are lower than normal. This presents good investment opportunities for contrarian thinkers. And even if inflation continues to trend downward, real estate must still be considered as an important vehicle to protect the purchasing power of pension and IRA assets.

Real estate clearly is a long-term investment—what makes it particularly pleasing to IRA owners is that it doesn't fluctuate in price every day the way stocks and bonds do. It has a record of consistent performance and is suitable for those IRA investors who don't want to move funds among a variety of investments, trying to guess the tops and bottoms of cyclical swings in the financial markets. Real estate also provides another avenue for portfolio diversification, the opportunity to add one more dimension to IRA holdings, and reduce the volatility of total returns.

CHAPTER 8

Managing the Self-Directed Account

Now that you've selected your investments and have an appropriate portfolio mix for your IRA, you need to concern yourself with properly managing it. The active IRA investor must always keep on top of his account (or accounts, if he has more than one), taking care of certain administrative matters in order to maximize returns. They include putting the investment holdings in some easy spreadsheet format for portfolio analysis, monitoring activity in the account, making rollovers and transfers among accounts, timing contributions, paying administrative fees, managing cash balances, and possibly even employing a little leverage.

Portfolio Analysis

You'll probably want to review the performance of your self-directed account at least annually and possibly even quarterly. If you've chosen the proper IRA investments, there's no need to watch them on a daily basis. In chapter 10, several performance measurement techniques are presented, ranging from rather sophisticated models to simple calculations. In order to work with them, you first must establish an accounting system for your IRA portfolio.

You should ask your advisor or broker for a periodic statement for your IRA funds, and he should be prepared to give it to you. If you're lucky, he or his firm may have developed a portfolio accounting system that will track your holdings for you. If you handle the IRA through a discount broker or have more than one account, then you must develop the figures yourself.

You can plug the relevant IRA statistics into your personal computer to aid in the portfolio management process. There are many canned portfolio management programs on the market which will run on the popular personal computers. Some can be telephonically hooked into data bases. The following are a few of the more popular programs in the $200 to $300 price range:

Financial Independence—	Charles Schwab & Co. 101 Montgomery Street San Francisco, CA 94104
Investment Manager—	International Microcomputer Software, Inc. 1299 Fourth Street San Raphael, CA 94901
Market Manager Plus—	Dow Jones & Company P.O. Box 300 Princeton, NJ 08540
Stock Portfolio System—	Smith Micro Software P.O. Box 7137 Huntington Beach, CA 92615
Stockpac II—	Standard & Poor's 25 Broadway New York, NY 10004
Wall Street Window—	R & D Software, Inc. P.O. Box 2727 Reston, VA 22090

The one you chose should accomplish what you want it to within your budget. Using modems and long distance telephone services, you can obtain current market values and yields and gain and loss figures on your IRA portfolio from one of several on-line information services. The largest and best known are Compuserve, the Dow-Jones News/ Retrieval, and the Source. This way, you don't have to search for the latest prices in the newspaper and make manual updates to your files.

However, you must perform a "cost-benefit" analysis to determine if going on-line is worthwhile for a small portfolio or one that's not heavily invested in stocks. If you already have programs to manage your regular portfolio, then it's not going to cost much to add a self-directed account or two. Generally speaking, the cost of portfolio software rises with the level of its sophistication. Going on-line can be expensive, and you need to control costs by logging on and off quickly and using the data bases at night and on the weekends to take advantage of lower rates.

You should consider several factors before reaching a decision on a portfolio analysis program to track your self-directed IRA holdings. Make sure the program sets up your records the way you like by putting on the computer screen what you would write out on paper. Ask certain questions including will the software access a large data base, account for stock splits, and show the latest dividend rates? Does it weight the portfolio for different types of investments? Will it figure taxes on securities transactions outside the IRA?

Obviously, you want the software to perform both IRA and non-IRA investment functions. With this in mind, make sure the software will handle multiple accounts on one diskette so you can easily compare portfolios. One of the most popular software programs gives automatic portfolio valuation updates, dividend distribution information, stock splits, holdings by portfolio segment, and links up with a data base.

An alternative to purchasing a software program is to take some time and program Lotus 1-2-3 to do the portfolio work for you. It will even give you graphic displays of your financial data. Simply set it up so you can categorize your investments into money market instruments, stocks, bonds, and other types of securities under the headings of equities and fixed incomes, consistent with the principles of portfolio allocation discussed in the previous chapter of this book. You may also want to subdivide further the categories depending on how many different investments are in your IRA.

Make the appropriate entries for the purchase price and current valuations, plus the annual dividend and interest payments, so you can calculate yields. You'll have to do it by hand, because 1-2-3 won't hook up to one of the major data banks unless you do some special programming.

Presented below is an example of how a 1-2-3 spreadsheet portfolio might look for the combined self-directed IRA holdings of a working couple who have made maximum contributions for four years. As can be seen, they have had modest appreciation in their portfolio, and earn a good current return from their holdings.

Investment	Cost	*Market* Value	*Percent* Change	Current Yield*	Percent of Total*	
Equity						43.1
Stocks	$ 4500	6000	33.3%	5.5%	22.9	
Mutual Funds	3000	5300	76.7	4.5	20.2	
Fixed Income						35.2
Money Market Funds	3000	3025	+0.8	7.5	11.5	
Mutual Funds	2000	2700	35.0	9.5	10.3	
Zero Coupon Bonds	2000	3500	75.0	11.0	13.3	
Real Estate						21.7
Limited Partnerships	2000	2000	—	7.0	7.6	
REITs	3500	3700	+5.7	7.5	14.1	
Totals	$19500	$26225	34.5	7.1%	100.0	100.0

* Based on market value.

If you prefer a simpler approach, take the data provided monthly, quarterly, or annually by your IRA trustee or custodian and make whatever calculations are needed using a hand calculator. If you have more than one self-directed account, merge them to obtain a composite of how your IRA investments stand.

In order to make some useful comparisons with other standard performance measures, you'll have to calculate the total value of your self-directed portfolio on an annual or quarterly basis. Figures should also be totaled for each heading category, if this is possible. You should print out the portfolio valuations at various points in time for comparison purposes. Otherwise, it will be extremely difficult to go back and run the numbers at a later date. And you'll need the year-end figures as a starting point for the following year's performance measurement. This is discussed in more detail in Chapter 10.

Monitoring Account Activity

One thing you should be on the lookout for is churning in your account, either by yourself or your broker. This is usually defined as excessive trading—more than 100% a year in a non-IRA and more than 25% in an IRA. You can calculate portfolio turnover by using the following formula:

$$\text{Turnover} = \frac{\text{Purchases During Year–\$2,000}}{\text{Beginning of Year Portfolio Value}}$$

Therefore, if you had $14,000 in your self-directed IRA at the beginning of the year and purchased $7,000 worth of investments, which includes the $2,000 annual contribution, your turnover would be:

$$\frac{\$7,000-\$2,000}{\$14,000} = \frac{\$5,000}{\$14,000} = 35.7\%$$

Although a bit on the high side, this would be an acceptable turnover for a moderately aggressive IRA investor. If your portfolio turns over more than this, then you should look at your goals and objectives and take steps to either change them or seek a new advisor. Remember, IRA investments should be held for the long term; very few people are successful short-term traders.

With proper monitoring of your self-directed IRA, you should be aware if the investment mix is still is consistent with your own personal goals and views on the state of the economy and financial markets. Also determine if your current portfolio is on target with your original intent, or any modifications made thereafter. Otherwise you need to change your goals and objectives or restructure the portfolio. Nothing is cast in stone forever.

Rollovers and Transfers

Rollovers and transfers are another important aspect of managing your self-directed IRA. The terms "rollover" and "transfer" often confuse people. Both activities involve shifting funds between qualified retirement plans, including IRAs. A rollover is accomplished by having the trustee of one IRA transmit funds to you, who then sends them to another IRA. With a rollover, you actually take possession of the cash and then have 60 days to place it in another IRA. If you don't reinvest the funds within this time span, then it's considered a deemed distribution subject to taxes and penalties.

On the other hand, the paperwork for a "transfer" of funds from one IRA to another is done between the two trustees. Transfers are the lazy person's method of having IRA funds switched. You never see the funds because the cash or securities are moved directly from one account to another. Unlike rollovers, the funds don't need to be transferred within 60 days to avoid penalties and taxes.

However, experience to date suggests that IRA transfers can take considerable time. This is particularly true during the first part of the year, when the back offices of trustees are extremely busy opening new IRA accounts and taking in IRA contributions. And transfers of limited partnerships take even longer because of additional paperwork required to re-register the interests in the name of the new trustee. Some may take anywhere from two to six months or even longer.

There have been numerous complaints about transfer delays, although many trustees and custodians have now speeded up the process. Remember, you have no control over a transfer once you authorize it. You may have a difficult time tracking down the paperwork that always seems to be somewhere between two trustees who are miles and miles apart. If you're not in a hurry, a transfer will work all right. But if the securities markets start to go against you, it may be better to rush things a bit by going the rollover route.

There is one other important difference between rollovers and transfers. Only one rollover can be made each year starting 365 days from the day you receive the funds, while an unlimited number of transfers can be made during that timespan. Actually, this will probably not be important for too many people because they should not have occasion to shift funds between IRA accounts very often. Again, IRA investments are for the long term.

When would you have an occassion to do a rollover or transfer? Suppose you have some funds in a bank certificate of deposit which are coming due soon. You know the rates on the next go around will not be as high as those available elsewhere. Therefore, you decide to add these funds to a newly established self-directed IRA where you can buy some higher-yielding zero coupon bonds. You have to move the funds out within a week after the CD matures; otherwise, the bank will automatically roll it over into another CD.

The simplist and quickest course of action is to go to the bank and fill out the appropriate paperwork to terminate your IRA account. You will receive a check for the proceeds, which can then be placed in into a new self-directed account. All you have to do is endorse the check over to the trustee of the new account, write a check for the fees, read and sign the plan adoption agreement, and have a broker execute the order for you. There is no waiting—this can all be done in one day.

Another situation might arise when you want to open an IRA to take advantage of a special situation which can only be bought through this new IRA. (Be wary of opening too many IRAs, as this could end up costing you a lot of money in setup and annual maintenance fees.) However, you don't have any funds currently available to make this year's IRA contribution, or you have already made the contribution. The best you can do is to use funds from an existing IRA to purchase the new investment. Through the use of the rollover mechanism, you can free up funds by withdrawing them from your IRA and endorsing the check over to the new trustee.

You may also want to roll over or transfer a qualified plan or 403(b) non-profit education institution pension plan into a self-directed IRA. The pros and cons of this type of rollover are discussed in the next chapter. Some IRA trustees require that if plan assets are liquidated, then they can only be rolled over after being distributed to the holder. If you want to retain the investments, then a transfer must take place. You should check with the trustee of your IRA before proceeding to liquidate assets in your pension plan.

If you have a complaint about the way a transfer or rollover from a mutual fund or a non-brokerage (i.e., independent) trustee is being handled, then contact the Securities and Exchange Commission, Department of Consumer Affairs, 450 Fifth Street NW, Washington, DC 20549. If the complaint is about a self-directed account you have with one of the brokerage firms, then direct it to the New York Stock Exchange, Department of Regulatory Services and Surveillance, 55 Water Street, New York, NY 10041.

Borrowing from Your IRA

Sometimes you might be hard-pressed for cash and decide to tap the IRA account for loan. You can't borrow directly for a long-term loan, for it will be deemed a distribution and will be subject to penalties and taxes. Nevertheless, you can make a short-term loan to yourself with a rollover and use the funds for sixty days as a "no interest loan." The thought is certainly tempting.

However, this is not recommended for several reasons. First, you lose the compounding of earnings effect when your funds are temporarily withdrawn from your IRA. Second, you can't be sure when the funds are going to reach you—the timing is in the hands of your trustee. Third, you have to be sure the funds will be returned to an IRA within sixty days; otherwise, you'll have to pay taxes and penalties on the withdrawal. If it turns out you need the loan for longer than sixty days, you could be in a bind.

Therefore, if you must borrow a few thousand dollars, it's best to go to your friendly banker or credit union administrator for a quick loan. Or margin securities in your regular investment account. Although you'll have to pay a high rate of interest, it's tax deductible and you won't jeopardize the tax-deferred compounding of earnings in your IRA.

Effect of Early Contributions

Proper IRA management dictates that if you have the funds, you should make your annual IRA contribution as soon in the year as possible in order to maximize earnings. Don't procrastinate. If you're in a high tax bracket, you might even borrow the funds to make the full contribution, then pay the loan off over the balance of the year or in the following year when you get your tax refund. The cost of a loan is tax deductible, while the funds compound tax free in the IRA. And that means your IRA is working harder for you to build your nest egg.

For example, if you can borrow at 10% and are in the 30% bracket, then your after-tax cost is only 7%. Investing these funds in your IRA may earn a conservative 10%, so you'll be three percentage points ahead of the game. And you'll have that many more dollars in your IRA compounding for you.

Another idea is to cash in some non-IRA investments and make the early contribution. If you have losses on them, then they can be deducted from your income. You can claim extra exemptions to lower the taxes withheld from your paycheck. In effect, you get a double deduction plus the advantage of more compounding, which gives grow power to the self-directed account.

Even if you don't have a specific IRA investment in mind, put the cash in the money market fund that the trustee of your self-directed account uses. At least it will be earning interest for your IRA for the maximum amount of time possible. As the table below shows, the differences in amounts accumulated by early January IRA investors, as opposed to later investors, are significant, assuming a 10% annual rate of return on funds in the account (the numbers are rounded):

	Date When $2,000 Contribution Made			
No. Years	*Jan. 1*	*June 1*	*Dec. 1*	*Apr. 15**
10	$ 35,000	$ 33,500	$ 32,000	$ 29,000
20	126,000	120,000	114,500	109,500
30	362,000	345,500	329,000	318,000

* Of the following year

The difference between a January contribution and one made on April 15th of the following year, just at the IRA contribution deadline, is $44,000 after 30 years. And these differences get considerably larger when returns higher than 10% are factored into the equation.

Paying Fees

With self-directed accounts as with other IRAs, you should pay your initial set-up charge and annual administrative fee by separate check. This will be considered by the IRS as an investment expense which can be deducted from your income taxes on Schedule A. In addition, you will have the maximum contribution compounding for you in your IRA because trustee fees have not been deducted from your account balances.

Unfortunately, some IRA trustees automatically deduct their fees before you have a chance to pay them. They don't bill you separately. Once the trustee has taken the fee, you've lost the deduction and you'll have a lesser amount of funds working for you. Check with the trustee to find out their policies in this regard.

Also, some trustees charge the annual fee for a calendar year, while others base it on a twelve-month period. There's no telling when the fee will be automatically deducted. It's best to mark the date down on your calendar to be sure you take the deduction by writing a separate check.

It's important to find out what the trustee charges for closing and transferring the funds to you or to another IRA. Often this can amount to $50 or more. Again, some trustees will automatically deduct this from your ending balance and send you a check for the difference. As with maintenance and other fees, the termination fee is also tax deductible on your 1040 form, so offer to pay the fee by separate check.

Managing Cash

In managing your self-directed IRAs, always try to maintain some cash in your accounts to take advantage of new investment opportunities that might come along. Likewise, maintain as much liquidity as possible in case you want to sell one of your less promising holdings in order to provide funds for the new investment.

If you have several self-directed IRAs and each has a small cash balance built up from dividends and interest payments, it may be a good idea to consolidate the funds so that investments in higher-yielding securities can be made. Presumably the idle funds will be invested in money market funds yielding short-term rates. You can combine funds by rolling the money market fund portion of each IRA into just one of the accounts.

The IRA account you should use to roll the cash balances into will be based on several criteria. The most important will be the next investment you anticipate making. If it's available from only one source through a particular self-directed account, then all other money market funds should be rolled to it. If it doesn't matter which IRA makes the purchase, then roll the funds to the account which has the largest amount of excess cash in it. The reasoning behind this is that when you roll funds over, you'll lose some interest when they're in transit. The funds are not issued by check drawn on the money market fund, but are from the trustee's account.

Leveraging Your IRA

Some persons may be interested in leveraging their IRA investments to try for maximum growth. IRA rules and regulations prohibit using margin accounts with an IRA. This effectively eliminates the possibility of leveraging stock and bond IRA investments to enable you to shoot for higher returns. Leverage cuts down on current returns because cash flows are used to service debt; on the other hand, leverage can magnify the capital gains potential of an investment. If you're interested in applying a little leverage to your IRA, you can accomplish this in several ways.

The easiest approach is to buy a limited partnership that employs leverage. You will want to purchase one that uses medium leverage (i.e., in the 30 to 50% debt/total capital range); otherwise you'll be losing a majority of the tax benefits in your already sheltered IRA. For this concept to work, you must have confidence that the assets will increase in value over the life of the partnership, so that you can capture the capital gain. For example, with a real estate limited partnership that employs 50% leverage, you can expect small but increasing cash flows of 2% to 4% in the early years, but good capital gains when the properties are eventually sold.

Another way to work a little leverage into your IRA portfolio is to buy common stocks of companies that are themselves highly leveraged. However, they won't be paying much in the way of dividends. But if their operating earnings increase, it will translate into higher profits per share which, in turn, could have a beneficial effect on the price of the stock. Natually, leverage is a two edged sword. If things go bad, they'll really go bad where leverage is used. With large fixed interest and principal obligations, the risk of company failure increases considerably.

Hopefully, you're now well on your way to managing successfully your self-directed IRA. The next chapter will cover your relationship with the Internal Revenue Service and its various forms, and other IRA-related situations which might arise in your quest for retirement security.

CHAPTER 9

Tax Forms and Other Issues

Congress enacted legislation that gave birth to the universal IRA. The Internal Revenue Service clothed it in rules and regulations and then fed it forms to keep it alive. Owners of self-directed IRAs are in about the same position as those with other types of IRAs when it comes to paperwork and tax forms. Naturally, if you own more than one IRA, then you may have additional work, but it's more a matter of keeping track of the extra trustee statements that come through the mail. You shouldn't have any difficulties unless you do a lot of rollovers, withdrawals, or inadvertently make an excess contribution.

There are several occasions when you'll come in contact with the IRS and its IRA forms. First, you need to put IRA contribution information on your 1040, or 1040A if you file this short form. This is as easy as putting down $2,000 on line 26 called "IRA deduction." In fact you should derive a great deal of pleasure from writing in the amount of $2,000, $2,250 or $4,000 as an adjustment to your income.

You will also have to put IRA rollover information on the Form 1040. Put the total received on line 17a and the portion that is taxable on line 17b. The IRS has developed some worksheets to help you figure out which part of distribution is taxable.

If you run into the problem of having made an excess contribution, a premature withdrawal, a prohibited transaction, or an excess accumulation, the IRS also has a separate form for reporting these more unusual transactions. It's called Form 5329, Return for Individual Retirement Arrangement Taxes.

As the name of the Form 5329 implies, you'll pay taxes if any of the above situations arise. This book will not go into detail on how to complete this form, other than to advise that you'd better fill it out and pay Uncle Sam any penalty taxes due.

The IRS requires all trustees and custodians to report IRA distributions on Form 1099-R. One copy goes to you and another to the IRS. Form 1099-R is called Statement for Recipients of Total Distributions from Profit Sharing, Retirement Plans and Individual Retirement Arrangements.

One of these 1099-R forms will be issued if you have a premature distribution, a rollover, a distribution because of disability or death, a prohibited transaction, a normal distribution, an excess contribution refunded (including any earnings on it) and transfer to spouse because of divorce. What you do with this information should be consistent with what you put on your Form 1040 and your Form 5329. The IRS wants you to leave a trail for where your IRA monies go. If they can't be tracked, then the revenuer's computers will start asking questions.

You shouldn't have any trouble dealing with the forms if you read the instructions carefully. And you can always ask your financial advisor or your IRA trustee or custodian how to interpret the information and then transcribe the numbers to the proper IRS forms.

The Pension Fund Rollover Issue

Those persons who change jobs or retire and receive a lump sum distribution from their qualified retirement plan have to decide whether or not to roll over the funds into an IRA. Only employer contributions can be rolled over; your voluntary contributions have already been taxed and aren't eligible for an IRA rollover. This decision to take a lump sum cash payment or to rollover the funds into an IRA is a difficult one for persons who are close to retirement and need the extra funds to support themselves. For others, the choice may be easier.

One special type of rollover is the "conduit IRA." This is used when you put your lump sum retirement plan distribution in a holding pattern after you switch employers. In order to make this work, you must place the distribution in a separate IRA, keep all the funds in it and make no further contributions to this conduit IRA. You can't commingle these funds with any other IRA funds. When the time comes to switch to another pension plan, terminate the conduit IRA and send the funds along.

The tax code provides a special advantage to those who take lump sum distributions from retirement plans. The funds are eligible for what is known as special "five-year income averaging" in calculating your tax liability. This works as follows: divide the lump sum distribution by five. Next, figure the tax on the resulting amount using single taxpayer tables. Then multiply this number by five to arrive at the total tax due the IRS for the lump sum distribution.

The tax resulting from five-year averaging is very low because, in effect, you assume that the lump sum was the only income received in each of the five years. For example, on a $40,000 distribution, the tax would be $6,000 for a person filing a 1987 joint income tax return. Treating the sum as ordinary income would result in a $14,000 tax ($12,100 in 1988 and beyond) just on the distribution for a married couple with $50,000 in taxable income, who are already in the 35% tax bracket (28% in 1988 and beyond) without taking into account the pension distribution.

As it turns out, notwithstanding this favorable tax treatment, you will usually be better off rolling your pension distribution into an IRA if you can spread the withdrawals over a long period of time. That's because the funds in the IRA will continue building up tax-free, and in a very short time you'll come out ahead with the IRA rollover. Continuing with the above example, a 10% rate of return was used for earnings, both inside and outside the IRA.

	5-Year Avg.	*IRA Option*
Original Distribution	$40,000	$ 40,000
Less: 5-year Avg. Taxes	6,000	—
Beginning Balance	34,000	40,000
Balance at end of:		
1 year	36,448*	44,000
5 years	48,134*	64,420
10 years	68,144*	103,750
15 years	96,472*	$167,070

* After taxes on earnings at the 28% rate.

With the IRA options, you are ahead by over $70,000, or almost 75% more than the amount you'd have if you were to take the five-year averaging. As the above example shows, if you're 15 years away from retirement and don't need the funds, the magic of IRA compounding will almost always result in a much larger retirement nest egg than paying the taxes using the five-year averaging method and reinvesting the funds outside the IRA where their earnings are taxed.

Even if you have to pay taxes on distributions from your IRA at the 33% level after 15 years, and you withdraw everything in one lump sum, you'll end up with 7.5% more than under five-year averaging ($112,104 versus $96,472). This includes the 15% penalty on lump sum distributions in excess of $112,500; without the penalty, you'd be ahead by 16%. But taking all the funds out of the IRA at one time is a most unlikely scenario. It's more likely you'll be in the 15 or 28% tax bracket, withdrawing a much smaller amount of funds from your IRA each year.

Some will take the five-year averaging alternative because they need the funds immediately. For instance, a middle-aged person who just left a corporation may use the funds to start up or buy an existing business because he has no other alternative other than to borrow or find equity capital from other sources. He can't afford to tie the funds up by rolling them over to an IRA.

You might think you can get the best of both worlds by taking the lump sum, paying the five-year averaging tax and then investing the difference in tax-free bonds. But this really restricts your investment flexibility. And if you're in a low bracket, you'd be better off with taxable bonds and higher yields. In addition, if your lump sum is sizable, then you may be hit with the 15% penalty on excess distributions, leaving a smaller portion to invest on the outside.

One more option is available. You can pay the five-year averaging tax and take the deferred annuity route on lump sum distributions. When you retire and take payments, only a portion of the income attributable to earnings on the annuity is taxed. However, this is better only if you know you will get high interest rates throughout the build-up and distribution phases of the annuity. Unfortunately, insurance companies are in a position to guarantee rates for only a few years.

For a lot of people, the addition of pension monies to the IRA will make it significantly larger. A $50,000 rollover into a $10,000 account will increase it by six times. With the bigness comes both problems and opportunities. The problem is that having worked and saved hard all these years to build these pension assets into a considerable sum of money, the tendency is to become over-conservative in their management.

The opportunities come from the ability to provide better diversification for your self-directed IRA and take advantage of a broader range of investment possibilities. With $60,000 at your disposal, you can invest in some rather illiquid partnerships that would not be available had you less funds. It will also enable you to develop your own portfolio of common stocks that best suits your needs.

In the final analysis, you'll have to work out the advantages and disadvantages of rolling over a lump sum distribution into an IRA. Your financial advisor can help with number crunching on his computer. However, once a decision is made (don't forget the rollover must be completed within 60 days), it's difficult to reverse. You can revoke your rollover decision without penalty before the due date of your tax return for that year (i.e., by April 15th of the following year). If you miss the deadline, you can still elect five-year forward averaging by filing an amended return and paying the 6% penalty and treating the rollover as an over-contribution to your IRA.

Keogh Versus Simplified Employee Pension Plan

One other type of pension plan relates to IRAs. Should a self-employed person set up a Keogh plan or should he put his retirement contributions into a Simplified Employee Pension plan, also known as a SEP? This latter funding mechanism allows self-employeds to combine their retirement contributions and IRAs into what is known as a SEP-IRA. In this way they don't have to create another, more complicated retirement plan, but can use their existing IRAs. Adding extra funds to the IRA gives it faster grow power.

As a self-employed person using a SEP, you don't have to be concerned with the paperwork connected with a Keogh—there's no IRS Form 5500-C to file by July 15th. This mandatory report is a rather confusing five pages long. It asks for information on your investments, income and expenses for your Keogh's most recent fiscal year. This reporting requirement was instituted to bring small pensions (single persons or over 10% owners) under the same rules as corporate pensions and large Keoghs. Fortunately the 5500-C is required only once every three years for those plans with more than one participant; in the intervening years a simpler update is all that's required.

An employer can also make SEP contributions directly to your IRA. The contribution is counted as additional compensation, but you can also take it as a deduction from gross income. Because annual contributions of up to 15% of net income, or $30,000, whichever is greater, are allowed for SEPs, your self-directed IRA can build quite fast under this arrangement. This allows you greater flexibility and diversification opportunities. All amounts eventually distributed from a SEP-IRA are taxed in full as ordinary income.

The biggest disadvantage of the SEP-IRA, compared to the Keogh plan, is that you can only contribute the lesser of 15% of your net income, or $30,000, whereas with the Keogh, you can contribute up to 20% or $30,000. So for those who are under the $30,000 limit and would like to maximize their contributions, they'll probably want to stick with the Keogh. Those who don't plan on contributing as large a percentage of earnings will be better off with the SEP-IRA.

Excess Contributions

There may be a time when you inadvertantly make an excess contribution to your self-directed IRA. One alternative is to carry the excess funds contributed before the end of the calendar year into the next and count this as part of your maximum $2,000 contribution. You must file form 5329 (discussed previously) with the IRS and pay 6% on the amount carried foward.

You can correct this error without having to pay the penalty. Don't deduct the excess from you income, but withdraw these funds from one of your IRAs plus any earnings on them, by the due date for your tax return. You won't be hit with the 6% penalty, but any earnings on the excess contributions will be subject to the 10% premature distribution penalty if you're under 59 and 1/2.

For example, suppose you inadvertently paid an extra $500 to your IRA and earned $35 interest on it. Right at tax preparation time you discover your mistake. Withdraw the $535 before you file your return and pay the $3.50 penalty on the withdrawn earnings (i.e., the earned interest). If it's difficult to determine what the amount earned on the excess funds was, then look at the earnings from various investments in your IRA and pick the lowest return. This way you won't over penalize yourself. You also need to check with your state tax authority to see if additional state income tax penalties apply.

One other alternative is available. You may have a valid excuse for having excess accumulations in your IRA. In this case, attach Form 5329 to your 1040 and pay the additional tax. But also send along an explanation and show what steps you've taken to correct and remove the excess. If the IRS approves your excuse, then you'll get your money back. Good justification for the error includes bad advise from your advisors or the fact that you didn't understand the formula. These reasons seem pretty broad. It appears the IRS will be fairly lenient towards excess contributions during these early years of the universal IRA.

CHAPTER 10

Measuring Performance of Your Self-Directed IRA

The last step in actively managing your self-directed IRA is to assess its performance. There's no reason why you can't handle this task the same way pension fund administrators do with monies under their control. Although your methodology may not be as sophisticated as theirs, with relatively little effort you should be able to arrive at a fairly accurate estimate of how well your IRA has performed.

Before beginning the assessment, you'll undoubtedly want to review the goals and objectives you set for the IRA at the time it was opened, along with any modifications made since then. These objectives could include bettering inflation by a certain percentage, beating the stock market averages by so many percentage points, or another quantifiable statement discussed back in Chapter 4.

Several questions arise when considering how to measure IRA portfolio performance. The first problem involves valuing the securities holdings. The second relates to the length of time for which performance should be measured. The third concerns the appropriate methodology to use. The final question is how sophisticated a measurement does one really need for an IRA?

It's important to get fairly accurate valuations of individual portfolio holdings by using the best available prices. All self-directed IRA trustees and custodians should provide you with annual statements of your account, including appropriate valuations, although they usually value limited partnerships at cost. Most other IRA investments trade in active securities markets, either on a national exchange or in the over-the-counter market. You can price them yourself or the IRA statement will show fairly recent prices. Look at the "bid," not "asked" side of the quotation if the securities don't trade on an exchange, or if you're valuing mutual funds, for this is the price you'd realize on sale.

Where possible, use the accrual basis of accounting by adding accrued income (earned but not received) of the IRA portfolio to the valuation. If individual bonds happen to make up a large part of your portfolio, be sure to include accrued interest on them. Bond interest is paid only twice a year, but will be a primary determinant of overall returns. Your financial advisor can calculate this accrued interest for you.

A more serious problem is trying to value limited partnerships, for they're not traded on a regular basis. Some partnerships, like real estate, will hopefully appreciate in value, while others such as oil and gas and equipment leasing usually decline as they mature and their assets deplete or depreciate.

If the cash flow from your real estate program has increased, then in all likelihood the value of your partnership interest has gone up by about the same percentage, assuming the capitalization rate (income divided by price) for real estate has remained the same. You also have to remember to subtract the general partner's cut on any potential profits before you value the partnership for portfolio purposes.

Some sponsors of real estate partnerships which are geared toward the pension market provide annual valuations to comply with the reporting requirements of the Employee Retirement Income Act of 1974 (ERISA). This makes the IRA portfolio valuation job much simpler, although it won't necessarily be a good indicator of how much you could sell the partnership for in the open market. As a last resort, value the partnership at cost unless it's one that is supposed to decline in value and has been in your portfolio for some time. In this latter case, mark it down by a small percentage each year.

It's best to calculate the total return on your IRA investments on an annual basis, which is a reasonable timespan for a long-term investment program. You don't want to measure results too often or you'll get into the performance syndrome, making judgments based on very short-term data. Annual valuations mean looking at portfolio asset values both at the beginning of the year and at the end of the year, assuming no funds were withdrawn without replacement.

Now that you've come up with some realistic valuation figures, you can begin to measure returns. Let's say your self-directed IRA had a beginning of the year balance of \$10,000 and a year-end balance of \$13,000. As shown in the formula below, subtracting one from the other and dividing the result by the beginning balance gives an exceptionally good annual return of 30.0%:

$$\frac{\text{End Value} - \text{Beginning Value}}{\text{Beginning Value}} = \frac{\$13{,}000 - \$10{,}000}{\$10{,}000}$$

$$= \$3{,}000/\$10{,}000$$

$$= .30 \times 100 = 30\%$$

So far, so good. However the question of annual contributions hasn't been addressed. Contributions made on January 1st or near the start of the calendar year should obviously be included as part of your IRA's beginning value by adding the appropriate contribution amount, usually \$2,000.

Needless to say, a complication arises in calculating IRA returns when the contribution was made at some other time during the year. In order to come up with a more accurate figure, you have to factor in when the new contribution was added to the account.

The time-weighted measure of performance is the preferred method for counting uncertain cash inflows. This eliminates the effect of timing and magnitude of external cash flows, or funds flowing in and out not subject to the fund manager's control. For most persons with IRAs, contributions will be made in one lump sum near the beginning of the year, regardless of whether they're for the current or previous calendar year. But some persons will spread payments throughout the year. In this latter case, these contributions should probably be lumped together and considered as paid in at the middle of the year in order to keep the measurement task simple.

Returning to the example above, if you made a \$2,000 contribution on April 1st, the IRA would have generated much less than a 30% return. That's because this \$2,000 was originally counted as part of your total return, whereas it was actually an addition of capital to the account. The revised formula shows the real return would have been only 8.3%.

$$\frac{\text{End Value} - \text{Beginning Value} - \text{Contributions}}{\text{Beginning Value} + \text{Contributions}}$$

$$= \frac{\$13{,}000 - \$10{,}000 - \$2{,}000}{\$10{,}000 + \$2{,}000}$$

$$= \$1000/\$12{,}000 = .0833 \times 100 = 8.3\%$$

However, we don't know if any of the 8.3% portfolio gain came before the contribution was made. This is significant, because it will indicate whether anything was earned on IRA during the first three months of the year. The time-weighted method of calculating returns helps answer this question. It adjusts for the timing and amount of cash flows. This method assumes you, the portfolio manager, have no control over the timing, although this is really not as big a problem for an IRA owner as it is for a pension fund administrator.

The time-weighted rate of return is calculated by measuring rates of return during a number of subperiods and then linking the interim returns. It's the average of the subperiod rates of returns. This sounds like a complicated procedure, but continuing on with the previous example will serve to clarify the concept.

In order to compute the time-weighted return, one must know the value of the portfolio the day before the contribution was made. Assume the value on March 31st was \$10,500, the value at the beginning of the year was again \$10,000, and year-end value was \$13,000. Therefore, for the first period, the rate of return was:

$$\frac{\$10{,}500 - \$10{,}000}{\$10{,}000} = \$500/\$10{,}000 = .05 \times 100 = 5\%$$

For the second period, the rate of return was the value at the end of the year (\$13,000), less the value at April 1, less the \$2,000 contribution, all divided by the April 1 value plus \$2,000. This is shown below as:

$$\frac{\$13{,}000 - \$10{,}500 - \$2{,}000}{\$10{,}500 + \$2{,}000} = \$500/\$12{,}500$$

$$= .04 \times 100 = 4\%$$

Linking the two together, the time-weighted return turns out to be a little better than 9%:

$$(1.05 \times 1.04) - 1 = .092 \times 100 = 9.2\%$$

The portfolio total return is now almost a full percentage point higher because a much lower base was used ($10,000 versus $12,000) in calculating returns for the first part of the year.

Of course you could have used an even simpler, but less accurate approach by taking the average account balance and dividing that into the returns:

$$\frac{\$1{,}000}{\frac{\text{End Value} + \text{Beginning Value}}{2}} = \frac{\$1{,}000}{\frac{\$13{,}000 - \$10{,}000}{2}}$$

$$= \frac{\$1{,}000}{\$11{,}500} = .087 \times 100 = 8.7\%$$

The return of 8.7% falls in between the unadjusted calculation and time-weighted measurement, as does the $11,500 base used to make the computations.

The time-adjusted formula and calculations are probably too cumbersome for persons with small IRAs. But it's one of the most accurate measurements available when there are capital inflows during the year. If you've followed what was said and went through the examples, then you're that much more informed as to the best method of calculating IRA portfolio returns, even though you may never actually use it.

If you want an easy way to calculate returns over several years, and you've made the full IRA contributions each year, then you can simply use the "Magic of Compounding" table in Appendix D for an approximation. This will give you annual compound rates of return. Go down the left-hand column to locate the number of years you've had your IRA. Then go across until you find a dollar amount that equates to the value of your portfolio. Read up the column to the heading to see what percentage annual return you've earned. If the figures aren't exact, then you can do some simple interpolation to arrive at a good approximation.

For example, if you've contributed $2,000 for five years running and your self-directed IRA is now worth $14,000, go down the table to the end of fifth year, move across the table to the amount $14,230, which is closest to the value of your IRA. Going up to the top of the table, you'll find the compound annual return is 12%. Because your total was slightly less than the $14,230 figure, your return was actually somewhere between 10% (the $13,431 figure) and 12%. Interpolating, the compound annual return comes out to about 11.7%, which is 70% between the two dollar amounts.

Once you've figured the rate of return on your self-directed IRA portfolio, you'll want to compare this with your goals and objectives. These may have been articulated in absolute terms such as achieving a certain percentage growth rate, or beating the inflation rate or the risk-free return on a Treasury bill by a fixed percentage. Or they may have included comparisons with standard market indices. In the latter case, an obvious problem arises if you have several investments in such diverse areas as the stock market, a money market fund, long-term bonds or real estate limited partnerships. How can you compare apples with pears and peaches? Is it fair to put the Dow-Jones Industrial Average or the Standard & Poor's 500 Stock Index up against your total portfolio when only a portion is in stocks?

Several market indicies can be used to compare how specific segments of your IRA portfolio performed. They will help explain total portfolio return and how it was achieved. The S&P 500 is a stock market indicator that's very popular with mutual fund managers, investment advisors and the people that track their performance. It's a group of 500 widely representative common stocks. The indicator assumes dividends are reinvested, and from it total return measures for different points in time can be calculated.

A yardstick used by fixed income investors is the Salomon Brothers High-Grade, Long-Term Corporate Bond Index. This index is based on a portfolio of long-term bonds (twenty or more years to maturity) of AAA or AA quality, and is calculated monthly. It may not match up perfectly with your IRA holdings, but will give a good approximation of how you're doing. It's a total return measurement, which includes current return plus appreciation or minus losses if the price of bonds has dropped.

Self-directed IRA investors may want to compare their returns from cash-equivalent instruments with the Donahue money market index, which tracks average yields of money market mutual funds. Another indicator to use is the three-month Treasury bill total return figure, the so-called riskless rate of return. However, there probably won't be much variance between your returns and those of these two indices, as these rates don't fluctuate widely within a short time period.

As far as returns on real estate are concerned, the Prudential PRISA index, mentioned earlier in the book, is about the most comprehensive one around. PRISA is an open-ended, commingled managed account of over $5 billion in a diversified group of 600 investment properties. But unless your general partner or trust manager provides annual valuations, it's pure guesswork trying to compare the performance of your real estate holdings with PRISA's. Also, the type and geographical location of the properties in your program may not match up well with the Prudential's.

You might also want to take into account the effect switching funds from one sector to another had on your portfolio. For example, if you had 70% in equities and 30% in fixed income for six months of the year, then switched to 50% equities and 50% fixed income for the rest of the year, the following returns would result if the bonds earned 8% in the first period and 7% in the second, and the stocks earned 5% in the first period and 12% in the second.

	First Period		*Second Period*		
Stocks	.70 × .05	+	.50 × .12	= .095	= 9.5%
Bonds	.30 × .08	+	.50 × .07	= .059	= 5.9%

The stocks averaged a 9.5% weighted return and the bonds 5.9% for the year. The overall portfolio earned 7.7%. However, results were penalized because of poor timing. When stocks were de-emphasized in the second half of the year, their returns went up; when the percentage of bonds was increased, their returns dropped. If the portfolio had stayed 70% invested in stocks and 30% in bonds thoughout the year, total returns would have been 8.2%, not 7.7%.

Finally, you might consider comparing the performance results of your IRA portfolio to managed funds of similar make-up. The previously-mentioned indicies, except for PRISA, were unmanaged groups of securities. You might match up the equity portion of your IRA with bank commingled managed funds, although these funds will always have a certain percent of cash equivalents in their equity portfolios. Computer Directions Services is a financial consulting firm which publishes the performances of the bank funds.

You could also compare your stock portfolio to the performance of various mutual funds that are equity-oriented and have objectives similar to yours. Likewise, you can compare your IRA's individual bond holdings to those of mutual funds that invest only in bonds. Many statistical services and publishers have performance figures for mutual funds, so the data is readily available.

With mutual funds in your portfolio, you'll naturally want to review their results against the performances of other mutual funds with similar portfolio composition and objectives. If your fund has not measured up to expectations, then you'll want to consider shifting to another fund. But remember, IRA and mutual fund investing are long-term propositions, so don't switch too often. Your particular fund may end up in the middle of the performance list one year, and at the top the next.

Before filing away your IRA portfolio calculations on rates of return to wait for the next performance measurement interval to pass, you should ask yourself and your advisors several very important questions related to risk. Were pre-established policies followed for acceptable risk levels for the IRA portfolio? And were actual returns achieved equal to, better, or worse than returns attributable to the risk level assumed?

In other words, were unacceptable risks taken to achieve the performance level attained? Perhaps the good results were due to a 75% investment in equities, when you really wanted less stock market exposure. If so, then there's a need to reassess investment objectives and policies. Were they sound to begin with and reasonable and obtainable? Could the desired returns have been achieved with a lower level of risk? These questions should be answered as part of the periodic IRA performance review. You want to monitor the complete investment strategy, which is based on your IRA objectives and tolerance for risk.

You or your advisors can look over your self-directed holdings to obtain a qualitative measurement of portfolio risk. Remember, risk relates to the level and variability of returns. You can review the chart in Chapter 7 to clarify the concept. Total portfolio risk will be a subjective evaluation of the mix of investments in it, and how each one relates to the others.

When it comes to performance measurement, don't pay too much attention to three-month returns for your self-directed IRA, or even one year's returns by themself. You need to take a longer perspective before making any wholesale changes in the way your IRA is managed or who is managing it. After three or four years, or the length of a complete business cycle, you should review results and consider your options.

In the final analysis, if you or your advisors are not at least beating inflation or staying even with some of the well-known market indices, then a change might be in order. You may need to relieve your advisor, or yourself, for that matter, and pick one that can help you attain the IRA investment goals and objectives you've articulated. This may be the most difficult decision of all, but certainly the most important one in terms of future IRA performance.

Remember, however, each time you fire your advisor (including yourself, if you're the IRA manager), you'll incur costs such as commissions for selling existing securities and buying new ones, and fees for closing IRAs and opening new accounts. And you may lose interest and dividends while your funds are in transit. Less earnings compounding on a tax-free basis can slow the speed of your IRA build-up.

* * * * * *

You should now be ready to actively manage your IRA the self-directed way. Close out those tired, old savings bank and money market IRAs and start putting your retirement dollars to work. If you follow the rules outlined in Chapter 2 of this book, you needn't worry about poor performance from your self-directed IRA. But you can't sit back and wait for it to grow into a large retirement nest egg—you must actively manage the account and continually search for profitable new investment opportunities.

The next several chapters provide some case studies of persons like yourself who need to fine tune their IRA programs to bring them more in line with their goals and objectives. The key ingredient for many of these people is fully utilizing the self-directed IRA with its built-in flexibility and investor control. They, like yourself, can finally take charge of retirement assets the old-fashioned way, by managing them to obtain the best returns available consistent with risks taken.

CHAPTER 11

Self-Directed IRAs for the Young Person

As a young person in the 25 to 40 year-old age bracket, your self-directed IRA portfolio should be weighted toward long-term growth. Naturally, the percentage of funds devoted to the growth objective will vary depending on your individual circumstances and personal preferences. On the whole, your self-directed holdings should be slightly more conservative than investments held outside the IRA. These are retirement funds you want to protect and preserve.

Three case studies of young persons and their IRAs are presented below. The first is of a young single man, the second of a working couple without children, and the third case study concerns a single parent. Each case is followed by recommendations on restructuring the IRA portfolio to make it more in line with goals and objectives and other personal circumstances of the IRA owner.

Single Person

Albert Martin is 28 and has been working for five years since his graduation from Georgetown University Business School. He's an assistant marketing manager with a medium-size consulting firm in the Washington, DC area. His current salary is $37,000 and he expects it to increase at a 7-10% annual clip as he moves into higher positions of responsibility with the firm. He has a pension plan with his company, but figures he can't count on it providing any retirement benefits, for he plans on leaving his current employer in a few years.

Al also believes he should settle down and get married when the right person comes along. He spends a lot of time and money dating, dining and traveling on the weekends. He eventually would like to move out of the apartment he's renting in Washington, DC, and buy a place outside the city. But he'll probably wait until he gets married before becoming a suburbanite.

Al has saved a few dollars since he began working. With his business school background, he considers himself a fairly sophisticated investor. He relies on a broker for recommendations on which stocks to buy. Al has $10,000 invested in companies that have good growth potential, but he has yet to make any money in the market. It seems that he has a tendency to buy stocks that are already fully priced *vis* á *vis* their long-term prospects. Al also owns a real estate limited partnership purchased several years ago to ease his tax burden. Except for his IRA contribution, he has virtually no other tax deductions available to him.

The first year Al opened an IRA, he put the $2,000 in a two-year certificate of deposit at a local bank, figuring that there was nothing else to do with such a small sum as far as making a meaningful investment was concerned. He has rolled this CD over every eighteen months since then.

The next two years he decided to put the IRA contributions in two different aggressive growth mutual funds, where he could aim for capital growth and at the same time reduce risk through diversification. He opted for dividend reinvestment plans with each fund.

The fourth year, his broker told him the best way to beat inflation with his IRA was to invest in a real estate limited partnership that was income-oriented, as opposed to tax-oriented. Al agreed and opened up a self-directed IRA with his broker's firm in order to make the purchase. Concerned about the risks of investing in the stock and bond markets, Al decided to put this year's $2,000 contribution into another bank certificate of deposit.

The total value of his IRA holdings is now $11,400 after five years of contributions. Al is not satisfied with this performance and wants to make some changes. Looking for more security and steady growth, he's starting to realize that if he begins job-hopping, he may not be able to count on a corporate pension when he retires. And Social Security benefits don't appear to be all that certain. Al figures that by adding up 30 to 35 years of IRA contributions, and getting a steady

12% return on them, his IRA will be worth over $500,000 and he'll be in pretty good financial shape when he finally hangs up his hat. He'll be more than content if he can achieve this objective.

His IRA holdings look like this:

Current IRAs of Albert Martin

Type and name	Date Purchased	Cost	Current Value	Current Yield
Fixed Income				
Bank CD #1	2/15/82	$ 2,000	$ 3,150	10.5
Bank CD #2	1/15/86	2,000	2,050	9.7
Equities				
Aggressive Growth Fund A	2/10/83	2,000	1,850	1.0
Aggressive Growth Fund B	1/ 9/84	2,000	2,350	1.3
Real Estate				
Income Fund	4/12/85	2,000	2,000	8.5
Total		$10,000	$11,400	

In analyzing Al's portfolio, several things are readily apparent. First, it's fairly well diversified between money market instruments, equities and real estate. This probably reflects his business school training. Second, part of it is oriented toward his objectives of long-term growth through the equity and real estate portions of the portfolio. These make up 55% of the total value.

One of the main negatives is that the portfolio is somewhat illiquid, with the certificates of deposit being subject to early withdrawal penalties and the limited partnership being completely illiquid (it could be sold, albeit at a deep discount from present worth). This limits his flexibility. The other negative is that too large a portion of the portfolio is weighted toward aggressive growth. Both mutual funds make risky investments in small, emerging high-tech companies.

What are Al's options? For one, he should consider adding funds to the self-directed IRA to take advantage of its investment potential. This can be accomplished by cashing in the bank certificates of deposit when they come due and rolling them over into the money market fund used by his brokerage firm's self-directed account. This will give him more investment flexibility and liquidity.

Secondly, he should sell the poorer performing of the two mutual funds (Fund A), and roll over the proceeds into his self-directed IRA. Then he should use $6,000 of the the $7,050 available to purchase a convertible bond fund or equity-income fund which would have high-yielding stocks with some growth potential. He should use $1,000 to buy shares in a good quality real estate investment trust. The balance of $1,050 should stay in the money market fund, with all dividends swept into it. That way, he will have ready cash to make other purchases when the right opportunities present themselves.

Al Martin's repositioned IRA portfolios would look like this on a combined basis:

Recommended IRA Portfolio Mix for
Albert Martin

	Percent Invested			
	Original		*Reposition*	
Fixed Income				
Short-term	46		9	
Long-term	0		0	
Total		46		9
Equities		37		65
Real Estate		17		26
Total		100		100

Al now has a higher percentage of the IRA portfolio in equities and real estate, but has not taken on much greater risk. This will give him more conservative growth consistent with his revised objectives.

Married Couple

Roy and Ann Morgan are a young couple in their late twenties who have been married five years. They live in a townhouse purchased three years ago in a pleasant suburb of Seattle, Washington. The Morgans met during college, dated for several years and then decided on a permanent relationship. Both work: Roy is a $33,000 a year architect with a small firm in Seattle, and Ann earns $35,000 as a lawyer on the corporate secretary's staff of one of the large forest products companies headquartered in the northwestern part of the United States.

The Morgans plan on having two children in the next five years.

They also know they'll need to move out of the townhouse into something larger when their family size increases. With a combined income of close to $70,000 in a part of the country with relatively low costs of living, Roy and Ann save about $10,000 a year. This is even after partaking in two of their favorite pastimes—eating out at the best local restaurants and traveling abroad several times a year.

Ann plans to continue in her job until she has children, and then will return to her company when the youngest reaches three. Roy plans to stay at the architectural firm until Ann resumes work. Then he'd like to join forces with a friend and start a new firm in downtown Seattle which specializes in commercial renovations.

The Morgans have amassed $40,000 as an investment kitty. They plan to use it for a larger house and for start-up expenses when Roy opens the doors of his own firm. They hope to live on Roy's salary while Ann is on leave with the children, although they probably won't be able to save anything during this time period. Right now their investment funds are in a money market fund, several growth mutual funds, and some individual tax-exempt bonds.

Both Roy and Ann participate in their company's pension plans, but are only partially vested. They expect that pensions, including a Keogh or other qualified plan that Roy establishes when he starts his own firm, will provide a good portion of their retirement income. They will not be totally dependent on their IRAs.

The Morgans are not very sophisticated in the ways of investing, but manage to read some of the popular business and financial magazines. They're basically conservative investors, but would like to change this approach as they become more familiar with the world of high finance. They picked their own no-load mutual funds, and bought the tax-exempt bonds through a local securities firm. Roy and Ann don't have a regular stockbroker, but are considering engaging the services of a financial planner to see them through the next five years.

Each of the Morgans has made four years of IRA contributions. They didn't contribute to an IRA in 1982, the first year they were available to every working person, because they had just started their careers and were saving for a down payment on their townhouse. Roy's IRA is now worth $9,250, while Ann's is valued at $9,500.

Roy and Ann invested their first two IRAs in bank certificates of deposit. They started out with fairly high interest rates locked in for a period of four years. Soon, several of the CDs will mature and the Morgans will be faced with a difficult reinvestment decision because new CDs are carrying much lower rates.

The next year the Morgans put their IRA funds into two different balanced mutual funds of the no-load variety. These funds have performed moderately well, generating relatively good income from the bond holdings and a small amount of unrealized capital appreciation from the stocks.

Most recently, with interest rates down, Roy and Ann decided to maximize their returns with a high-yielding mutual fund that invests in junk bonds. They feel this will provide them a much better yield than they could get from a bank CD or money market fund. Their current IRA holdings are as follows:

Current IRAs of Roy and Ann Morgan

Type and name	*Date Purchased*	*Cost*	*Current Value*	*Current Yield*
Fixed Income				
Bank CD #1–3 years (Both)	7/18/83	$ 4,000	$ 5,750	13.5
Bank CD #2–3 years (Both)	1/ 5/84	4,000	5,000	12.5
High-Yield Fund (Both)	2/10/86	4,000	4,200	13.0
Equities				
Balanced Fund A (Roy)	1/12/85	2,000	2,250	6.0
Balanced Fund B (Ann)	1/12/85	2,000	2,400	5.5
Total		$16,000	$19,600	

It's clear the Morgan's IRA portfolio has a conservative bent to it, with most of the assets in fixed income securities, and a small portion in equities through ownership of the balanced funds. Although the portfolio is heavily weighted toward fixed income, they've achieved a measure of diversification, and their holdings are mostly short-term, so they're not subjecting themselves to interest rate risk.

Their biggest worry is with the high-yield mutual fund, which could go down in value if interest rates increase. And this bond fund would be even more volatile if the rate spread between junk bonds and the highest quality bonds happened to widen.

The Morgans should become a little more aggressive with their IRA investments, knowing they have a long ways to go before retirement and both plan to continue work until that time. A little aggressiveness now will pay off in a larger nest egg later on. The Morgans are also leaving themselves short when it comes to protecting their IRA assets against future inflation.

One further observation. The Morgans have all their IRA interest and dividends reinvested in the stock and bond mutual funds, even though they could have the distributions swept into a money market fund. They're not accumulating cash balances for further diversification. Also, the Morgans have six separate IRAs (three each) which might be reduced in number to save on administrative fees.

The Morgans should combine their separate IRAs when it comes to portfolio management—together they have a total of almost $20,000 in them. They don't need to duplicate each other's IRA investments but should spread them around for more diversification.

The Morgans should hold on to the CDs until maturity because they're throwing off good yields for short-term securities and the penalties for early withdrawal are harsh. Roy should liquidate his lesser performing balanced fund. Finally, both should sell their shares in the high-yield bond fund.

With $20,000 between them, they should each consider opening up self-directed IRAs. Roy can put the proceeds from the sale of the balanced fund and high-yield fund into it. When the first CD matures, the proceeds should be added to the reinvestment kitty. With $7,000, he can direct his broker to come up with several high-yielding stocks with growth potential, and recommend a $2,000 real investment (a trust or an income-oriented limited partnership). Although three to five stocks may be considered too risky, if the investments are in blue-chip companies with good dividend paying histories, they should not be too volatile. Also, these holdings will represent only one-quarter of the value of the combined portfolios. As Roy's IRA grows, additional stocks may be purchased.

After opening a self-directed IRA, Ann should consider placing half her $5,000 realized from the sale of the CD and the high-yield bond fund in a convertible bond fund and the other half in medium-term zero coupon government bonds. This will provide a chance for some capital appreciation along with good yields and stability of capital.

The new Morgan IRA portfolios would look like this, on a percentage of asset basis, assuming the balanced fund is invested one-half in long-term bonds and the other half in stocks:

Recommended IRA Portfolio Mix for
Roy and Ann Morgan

	Percent Invested			
	Original		Reposition	
Fixed Income				
Short-term	55		26	
Long-term	33		19	
Total		88		45
Equities		12		45
Real Estate		0		10
Total		100		100

The net effect is to give the Morgans' combined IRAs a more growth-oriented focus through the increase in equity ownership from 24% to 51% of the portfolio. Plus the addition of real estate provides another avenue of capital growth and some inflation protection. And the zero coupon bonds are less risky than the junk bond fund. As the remaining CDs mature, part of the proceeds can go into the money market fund and the balance into the equity and real estate portions of the portfolio.

A Single Parent

Betty Wright is 33 years old with two children. Two and one-half years ago she divorced her husband of ten years and now she's going it alone in a suburb of Chicago. Betty has been working for three years as a clothing designer at a small garment firm in the Windy City. Her children, aged five and seven, attend public schools in Wilmette and go to an after-school day care program. Betty is hoping to remarry, but doesn't believe this will happen soon.

In her divorce settlement, Betty got the house and $750 a month for child support, which increases each year in step with the cost of living. She feels she can count on these payments, because her ex-husband has a steady job and is a responsible person. In the division of property, she received no assets other than the house and furniture and part of her former husband's IRA. Both she and her ex-husband will share college education expenses for the two children.

Betty's salary currently is $28,000. It's expected to increase at a fairly good pace, because she has an obvious flair for design. Her company takes good care of her by providing an excellent fringe benefit package. She expects to stay for quite some time.

Betty's biggest expenses are a $700 a month mortgage payment and $5,000 a year in child care expenses. She has had to cut back on her family's standard of living. Right now, Betty is saving to build up an emergency fund. She figures that in several years her increased salary plus a cutback in child care costs when the children get older will enable her to start an investment program. She's definitely interested in financial matters, because her father is a retired insurance salesman. She thinks she can do better with her IRA investments and would like to point it in the direction of more growth.

Betty's former husband had contributed $250 a year to her spousal IRA for two years before their divorce. She also received $2,500 from his IRA, which was transferred to her at the time of the divorce. All $3,000 plus $750 in accumulated interest earnings have been sitting in a savings bank IRA, invested in certificates of deposit.

Since she started working, Betty set up her own IRA with a money market mutual fund. She believes in the savings ethic and thinks that IRAs are a good way to build net worth for retirement because the earnings accumulate tax-free. The first year she made a $1,500 contribution and the next two years she put aside the full $2,000. Betty has $167 deducted from her paycheck each month and sent to the mutual fund, figuring it's easier to save that way. Betty's current IRA investments of almost $10,000 look like this:

Current IRAs of Betty Wright

Type and name	*Purchased*	*Cost*	*Value*	*Yield*
Fixed Income				
Bank CD–2 years	Various	$3,000	$3,750	11.5
Money Market Fund	Various	5,500	6,000	7.5
Total		$8,500	$9,750	

As is evident, all Betty's IRA funds are tied up in money market-type investments. She's subject to the ups and downs of short-term interest rates, but her principal is well protected. This is a good position to be in if she ever needs to tap the funds for an emergency, although she'll pay interest penalties if she has to cash in the CDs prematurely.

In order to begin diversifying the IRA portfolio as it grows, Betty should look at some alternative investments possibilities. She should consider opening up a self-directed IRA and purchasing $3,000 worth of medium-term zero coupon government bonds. She would lock up relatively high yields without having to worry about the credit-worthiness of the issuer. Betty might also add some growth potential to her IRA by putting $2,000 in an equity-income or balanced mutual fund.

Recommended IRA Portfolio Mix for Betty Wright

	Percent Invested			
	Original		*Reposition*	
Fixed Income				
Short-term	100		48	
Long-term	0		31	
Total		100		79
Equities		0		21
Real Estate		0		0
Total		100		100

Betty's repositioned IRA portfolio is now spread between short and long-term fixed income securities, with a small portion in the equities markets. This makes for a good transition to the slightly more aggressive investment posture that she wants to take.

Because she plans to continue working, she'll make the full IRA contributions each year. This will enable her to take some risks now, knowing full well there will be a steady supply of new funds coming into the IRA in the future. As her emergency fund and outside investments build up, she could also consider purchasing some real estate to provide steady income and growth and a hedge against inflation. Because this is not liquid, she shouldn't purchase it now when there is the slightest possibility of her needing to liquidate IRA funds in a hurry.

CHAPTER 12

Self-Directed IRAs for the Middle Age Person

Your self-directed IRA portfolio should probably still be oriented toward growth, but not quite to the same extent as a younger person's IRA. The degree to which a middle age person (i.e., in the 40 to 55 year age bracket) will be less conservative depends on the amount of assets held outside the IRA, the number of years to retirement, and the size of the IRA itself.

At this stage in life, the more a person feels he will be dependent on the IRA for a major part of retirement fund needs, the more conservative his investment approach should become. The emphasis should center on securities with medium to high levels of current income that also provide some capital growth to offset the effect of inflation on the purchasing power of the IRA dollars.

Several case studies of middle-age persons and their IRAs are presented below. The first case describes a couple where only the husband works, the second where both husband and wife work, and the third case is of a single man without any family. Recommendations on IRA portfolio repositioning follow each case.

One Working Spouse

John and Susan Hammond live in Paoli, Pennsylvania, a suburb of Philadelphia. John is vice president of a large electric utility company in the "City of Brotherly Love" and Susan is a housewife. John is 45 and Susan is three years younger; they have two children, both of whom attend private colleges in the northeast.

John's salary is $75,000 a year, but with two children in college, he needs to borrow to meet expenses. The Hammond's assets, outside their IRAs and home equity, are in a money market mutual fund and a small bond fund. They have given most of their savings to the children to pay for their college costs, which run around $25,000 a year. The girl will graduate in one year and the son has three years to go.

The Hammonds aren't saving any money at the moment, as Susan chose not to go back to work to help pay college expenses. She reasoned that because they were in such a high income tax bracket, her earnings would only be taxed away at the margin, leaving little extra discretionary income. She also did not want to give up her heavy load of volunteer work in the community.

John has diligently made his IRA contributions every year since they became available to all workers. He also makes the $250 spousal contribution into Susan's IRA. The total value of his portfolio is almost $14,000; that of his wife is $1,750.

Because he feels he can rely on a good pension from his employer, John has been willing to take some risks with his IRA investments. He hopes to work fifteen more years and then retire at age 60. Also, he knows that when the children are finished with college and the loans paid off, he and Susan will start accumulating other assets for retirement. In short, the Hammonds probably won't be depending on the IRAs for a large part of their retirement needs. They would like their IRAs to grow as fast as possible to help build up their estate for the children.

Like many other individuals, John invested his first IRA in a money market mutual fund when interest rates were in double digits. He also put the $250 for Susan's spousal account in a money market fund, and each subsequent $250 contribution has been added to the fund. The second year he opened up a self-directed IRA with one of the national brokerage firms and bought long-term zero coupon bonds because he wanted to lock in very good rates. John plans to hold these for a number of years, even after he retires.

Thinking the stock market was a good place to be, he put his third year's IRA contribution into a growth fund with the same mutual fund management company that had his other small, non-IRA investments. The fourth year the stockbroker convinced him he ought to buy a limited partnership that invests in real estate mortgage loans with equity kickers. This purchase was executed through the same self-directed IRA that holds the zero coupon bonds.

John has just made his most recent year's contribution to the money market fund used by the brokerage firm for its customers' self-directed IRAs. He wasn't sure what to invest it in and his broker had no recommendations that seemed worthwhile at the moment. Dividends and distributions from his IRA investments are swept into money market accounts.

The Hammond's IRA portfolios look like this:

Current IRAs of John and Susan Hammond

			Current	
Type and name	*Date Purchased*	*Cost*	*Value*	*Yield*
Fixed Income				
Money Market Fund (John)	2/15/82	$ 2,000	$ 3,000	8.5
	2/10/86	2,000	2,500	8.5
Money Market Fund (Susan)	Various	1,250	1,500	8.5
Zero Coupon Bonds (John)	1/18/83	2,000	2,400	12.5
Equities				
Growth Fund (John)	2/10/83	2,000	2,550	3.0
Real Estate				
Mortgage Fund L.P. (John)	2/12/85	2,000	2,000	10.5
Totals		$11,250	$14,550	

The problem with John's portfolio is that it's too heavily weighted toward fixed income securities. In fact, counting his wife's spousal IRA, about 70% of the funds are in interest-sensitive investments. Of this, 72% is in money market funds subject to the vagaries of short-term interest rates. One month the portfolio might be earning fairly good returns; six months later rates could drop considerably. This may be a good temporary position to be in if he feels defensive about other investments, but it's not a good long-range investment policy.

John should reposition his portfolio assets to make their composition more consistent with his growth objectives. He should consider using $2,500 of money market funds to add a convertible bond fund to his self-directed IRA through the purchase of one of several closed-end funds available in the secondary market. This will give him relatively high current income with a chance for capital appreciation if the stock market heats up. He also might use another $2,500 to add a balanced fund or an equity-income fund to the portfolio to provide not only relatively high current income but also some capital gain potential.

John might also consider having the dividends from the growth fund plowed back into the fund, rather than be swept over to the money market fund. He should also transfer the growth fund into the brokerage firm self-directed IRA, and then make periodic share purchases with funds from the money market account as this builds up with distributions from the various mutual funds. This will allow him to "average out" share cost, buying less shares when the price is up and more when the price is down. Bringing the fund under the self-directed umbrella will also save one trustee's annual administration fee.

The initial portfolio changes will orient the Hammond's IRAs more toward the growth side of the investment equation, while still leaving them with several fixed income investments to provide pure yield and reduce overall portfolio risk. Here's how the Hammond IRA portfolio would look after repositioning:

Recommended IRA Portfolio Mix for John and Susan Hammond

	Percent Invested			
	Original		*Reposition*	
Fixed Income				
Short-term	50		15	
Long-term	19		20	
Total		69		35
Equities		17		52
Real Estate		14		13
Total		100		100

As a result of these portfolio switches, the Hammonds now have slightly over 50% of their IRA funds in the equity markets (including convertible bond and equity-income funds). The money market portion has dropped to 15%, which still provides a cushion in the event the stock market weakens. And it allows them to make another investment should a very promising one come along. Further down the road, when Susan's spousal account builds up, this might be invested in a medium-term fund to provide more yield.

Two Working Spouses

Paul and Martha Bowman are a professional working couple living in New York City. They have a 19-year old son who just began college at Cornell University. The Bowmans own a cooperative apartment in upper Manhattan. Both work in the Big Apple; Paul is a partner in a medium-size law firm in the midtown area, while Martha is self-employed as a commercial artist.

Paul, who is 52, makes $110,000 a year. His firm has a qualified pension plan which he will tap into upon retirement at age 65. Martha, age 49, earned $65,000 last year from her business. She started her company five years ago when their son began high school; however, she does not know how much longer she will continue working. Martha has a Keogh plan to which she contributes the maximum 20% of her self-employed earnings. Half of the $30,000 in her plan is invested in a money market fund, and the other half in a high-yield bond fund.

Despite high taxes and cost of living in New York City, the Bowmans have been able to stash away considerable sums of money. They have $275,000 in investments, including $100,000 in tax shelters. In addition, they've gifted enough funds to their son to pay for all his college expenses.

The Bowmans consider themselves fairly aggressive investors. Through their financial planner, they have purchased several growth mutual funds and New York State tax-exempt bonds in addition to the highly leveraged private placement real estate deals. They expect to continue investing in tax-advantaged investments as long as their tax bracket remains high.

Naturally, the Bowmans have made the most of their IRA deductions, contributing the maximum amounts ever since the universal IRA came into being. Together, their IRAs have grown to almost $25,000 in value. They established self-directed IRAs with their financial planner, and each year both Paul and Martha make the same investments; in fact, their IRA portfolios are almost exactly alike.

Each includes income-oriented real estate limited partnerships, growth funds, and zero coupon bonds.

The IRA portfolios, on a combined basis, look like this:

Current IRAs of Paul and Martha Bowman

Type and name	Date Purchased	Cost	Current Value	Current Yield
Fixed Income				
Money Market Fund (Both)	Various	$ 1,750	$ 1,750	8.0
Zero Coupon Bonds (Both)	1/18/82	4,000	5,800	12.5
Equities				
Aggressive Fund (Both)	2/10/83	4,000	4,500	1.0
Real Estate				
Income-oriented #1 (Both)	2/12/84	4,000	4,500	9.5
Income-oriented #2 (Both)	1/18/86	4,000	4,000	7.5
REIT (Both)	3/15/85	4,000	4,100	9.0
Total		$21,750	$24,650	

The Bowmans have achieved some diversification, but their combined IRA portfolio is obviously heavily weighted toward real estate. This is even more apparent when investments held outside the IRA are taken into consideration. The Bowmans should consider diversifying more into the equity markets. They could do this by selling the real estate investment trust (the partnerships are too illiquid to dispose of at a reasonable price) and combining the proceeds with money market funds to purchase an international fund. This would provide a more diversified approach and offset risks in the U.S. equities markets. As shown below, this would drop the real estate percentage from about one-half to one-third and raise the equity portion from 18% to 42%.

In addition, the Bowmans should consider liquidating the aggressive growth fund and put the funds into an income-oriented fund. This appears to be more appropriate for them at their stage in life—they don't need to go for pure capital gain in an IRA. They should not put additional limited partnerships in their IRAs because these type of investments are too long-term oriented for persons close to retirement.

Factoring in the above changes, the revised Bowman IRA portfolio would look like this:

Recommended Portfolio Mix for
Paul and Martha Bowman

	Percent Invested			
	Original		*Reposition*	
Fixed Income				
Short-term	7		0	
Long-term	24		24	
Total		31		24
Equities		18		42
Real Estate		51		34
Total		100		100

Another possibility is for Martha to switch her Keogh into a Simplified Employee Plan (SEP-IRA). Her combined funds of $42,500, plus the $12,500 in Paul's IRA, total $55,000. This would enable them to begin purchasing a small group of high-yielding individual stocks for the portfolio. But with a SEP-IRA, Martha would only be able to deduct 15% instead of 20% from her net income before figuring taxes. She would lose some of the shelter provided by the Keogh.

Single Person

David Gumport is a single person age 45 who has never been married. He enjoys being a bachelor and probably will never share his life with another person on a permanent basis. He owns and manages a successful restaurant in Baltimore, Maryland. David lives in a rental apartment in a pleasant residential section of the city, not too far from the restaurant. He enjoys the luxury of a short walk to work.

David takes out $55,000 a year from the 75-seat capacity restaurant, but the hours are long. Most business is at dinner time, although the eatery does have a limited menu luncheon for the business crowd. David developed many of the continental cuisine entrees by experimenting with various ingredients over the years. The restaurant is open six days a week from about 11:30 in the morning until midnight each day. David doesn't have much time for financial matters other than running the business. His accountant provides most of his personal financial advice.

With his accountant's assistance, David set up a profit-sharing plan for himself and his staff at the restaurant. He likes running the business with a "family" of employees sharing in its success, and especially wants to keep the chief cook and head waiter on the staff for as long as possible. However, very few other persons are vested in the plan because of the rapid turnover of waiters, waitresses, and kitchen help. David's pension plan account now amounts to $65,000. It's invested in a family of mutual funds, with about one-half in a long-term bond fund and the other-half in a balanced fund.

His other main asset is the restaurant, which his accountant values at about $300,000. Lately, the business has not been expanding because of size limitations of the current location. David is considering relocating to a larger facility or starting another restaurant. However, his first love is good food and his second is happy customers; he doesn't want to expand the business just to put more dollars in his pocket.

David's fantasy is to retire in about ten years, sell the restaurant and move to a Greek island. If this doesn't work out, he's also contemplated writing travel articles on the best gourmet restaurants all over the world. Either way, he feels at age 55 he'll be ready for a major lifestyle change.

David has been contributing to his IRA since it was first offered as a universal retirement account in 1982. It's now worth a bit more than $12,000. For the first year, his accountant advised putting the IRA contribution in a money market fund. The next year, David bought a growth mutual fund of the no-load variety that his accountant recommended because of its good track record. The third year he opened a self-directed IRA and bought some zero coupon bonds which mature in the year just before he reaches age 59 and 1/2. The fourth year he bought some more zeros—David likes the idea of paying only a fraction of their face value and watching them grow. This year's IRA contribution is sitting in a money market fund waiting for interest rates to go up.

David's current IRA portfolio appears on the following page.

David's pension plan is set up with a large mutual fund company as trustee. Each plan participant controls how he wants his money invested. Although David and his employees can chose between money market funds, bond funds and stock funds, they are limited to these

Current IRAs of David Gumport

Type and name	Date Purchased	Cost	Current Value	Current Yield
Fixed Income				
Money Market Fund	Various	$4,000	$5,000	7.5
Zero Coupon Bonds	1/18/84	2,000	2,500	12.5
	2/12/85	2,000	2,225	12.0
Equities				
Growth Fund	2/10/83	2,000	2,500	1.0
Total		$10,000	$12,225	

choices and can't invest retirement funds anywhere else. The accountant advised this was the easiest route to take for a small plan with more than one participant. Everyone has the same investment alternatives and all administrative chores are handled by the mutual fund's plan custodian.

David should consider his pension plan and IRAs together as one investment portfolio, because these are his two main retirement funds and he controls them both. Although he can count on the sale of the restaurant business for additional capital to use in retirement, he should not depend too heavily on this source. First of all, he doesn't know what it will be worth in ten years. Secondly, he'll need to use some of the sales proceeds for living expenses between the time he retires at age 55 and the time he begins withdrawing funds from the pension plan (if he hasn't rolled it into the IRA before then) without penalty.

David's combined portfolios are depicted on page 178.

When considered together, the portfolio has a good mix of stocks and fixed income investments. One area that is absent is real estate. In this regard, some of the IRA money market funds can be used to buy a limited partnership or real estate investment trust to round out the portfolio.

Half the long-term bond fund monies should be switched into a short to medium-term bond fund (less than five years average maturity) in the pension plan family of funds. This would lower yields somewhat, but would also reduce David's exposure to interest rate risk which clearly exists as long as such a large percentage of assets are tied up in the long-term bond fund.

Current Combined IRA and Pension Plan Account for David Gumport

Type and name	*Date Purchased*	*Cost*	*Current Value*	*Current Yield*
Fixed Income				
Money Market Fund	Various	$ 4,000	$ 5,000	9.5
Zero Coupon Bonds	1/18/84	2,000	2,500	12.5
	2/12/85	2,000	2,225	12.0
Long-term Bond Fund (Pension)	Various	27,000	33,000	11.5
Equities				
Growth Fund	2/10/83	2,000	2,500	1.0
Balanced Fund (Pension)	Various	29,000	32,000	5.5
Total		$66,000	$77,225	

A repositioning of these retirement fund assets would result in the following percentages of asset mix:

Recommended Portfolio Mix for David Gumport

	Percent Invested			
	Original		*Reposition*	
Fixed Income				
Short-term	6		21	
Long-term	49		27	
Total		55		48
Equities		45		45
Real Estate		0		7
Total		100		100

By following these recommendations, David would have only 27% of total retirement assets in long-term fixed income investments. In addition, he adds real estate to his portfolio to give it another dimension. Future IRA contributions might also go into this category to build the percentage up to at least 10 or 15%. Without wife or dependents, David Gumport will be concerned only with taking care of himself during retirement. He can afford to take some carefully measured risks with his self-directed IRA.

CHAPTER 13

Self-Directed IRAs for the Older Person

As you near retirement or finally end a working career, your self-directed IRA investments should be oriented toward conserving principal, maintaining adequate liquidity, and producing satisfactory current income. A lot will depend on your personal circumstances aside from the IRA. That is, how large a pension will you receive, and how large is your net asset base apart from the IRA? If the answer to one or both of these questions is "large," then you can afford to be a little more aggressive with your IRA funds than the average senior citizen. If the answer is "small," then you must position your IRA portfolio on the more conservative side of the investment fence.

The worst trap is to become hooked on fixed income investments in your retirement years. Your IRA dollars could be destroyed by inflation. If you're a male and retire at age 62, you still have almost 17 years of life expectancy; women at that age have over 20 years. This is a long time for inflation to take its toll on the purchasing power of your retirement dollars. You want to protect yourself against this possibility without unduly risking your hard-earned funds.

Several case studies of older persons and their IRAs will be presented below. The first is of a couple where the husband works and will retire in three years. The second concerns a retired couple that don't need to depend on their IRAs for retirement income. The third case study is of a widow who must count on the IRA for retirement income.

Couple Near Retirement

Fred and Sally Lawrence live in Dallas, Texas, where Fred works as vice president of a local grocery store chain. He spent many years with this company, starting out as a stock boy after graduation from high school. The Lawrences have three grown children, all of whom are married and raising their own families.

Sally, age 60, worked for several years after she and Fred were married, but stopped when the first child was born. Fred is 62 and plans to retire in three years. He currently makes $35,000 a year, but expects to receive a $20,000 annual pension. This, plus Social Security benefits, will be enough for the Lawrences to live comfortably on. They plan to continue residing in their home in Dallas to be near their children and grandchildren.

The Lawrences have not been able to accumulate any meaningful amount of capital outside their home equity. Although they live modestly, Fred and Sally spent many years supporting their kids through college and post-graduate schools. This has taken a toll on their net worth. However, they're very proud of their children's accomplishments and are glad for the sacrifices made.

Fred and Sally have little experience with investments. The $15,000 they've saved outside their IRA is split equally between a money market mutual fund and Ginnie Mae bond fund. They heard about these investments from one of their neighbors, who is also recommending a real estate limited partnership which makes wraparound mortgages that throw off high yields.

The Lawrences are conservative by nature and have invested their IRA funds accordingly. The accounts now total $13,000. When Fred retires, they should be worth around $20,000. At that juncture, he may work part-time to put additional funds into the account until he reaches age 70. He's a firm believer in the value of an IRA, and only wishes they'd been available to everyone many years earlier.

Fred and Sally figure on using their IRAs as emergency funds during their retirement years. If they aren't completely withdrawn by the time both die, then the balances will become part of the children's inheritances. This is fine with the Lawrences.

Fred put his first year's IRA contribution of $2,000 in a three-year bank certificate of deposit when interest rates were high. He put the $250 contribution for Sally's spousal account in a money market fund at the bank, and has done the same in each ensuing year. Fred always makes his IRA contributions one year later at the time he prepares his income tax forms.

Because interest rates were high at the time, he put his second and third year IRA contributions into bank CDs. For the 1985 contribution, he decided to buy a high-yield bond fund through the same family of funds that runs his Ginnie Mae fund. He opened an IRA with the fund's custodian bank. It had a better yield than any available bank CD. Monthly dividends are plowed back into more shares of the fund.

The Lawrence's IRA portfolios look like this:

Current IRAs of Fred and Sally Lawrence

			Current	
Type and name	*Date Purchased*	*Cost*	*Value*	*Yield*
Fixed Income				
Money Market Fund (Sally)	Various	$1,000	$ 2,000	8.0%
Bank CD #1 (Fred)	2/15/83	2,000	2,750	12.5
Bank CD #2 (Fred)	3/15/84	2,000	2,500	11.7
Bank CD #3 (Fred)	2/20/85	2,000	2,200	10.5
High-yield Fund (Fred)	3/1/86	2,000	2,075	11.8
Total		$9,000	$10,725	

Several recommendations are in order. First, Fred should make every effort to put his annual contribution in his IRA at the beginning of the year, so the earnings will compound for a longer period of time. Second, he should have the dividends from the high-yield fund go directly into a money market fund. Although the high-yield fund provides him with a good return, these funds typically invest in lower-grade securities and there is a risk of principal loss. By not having dividends reinvested, greater diversification possibilities will be created for his portfolio.

The following recommended portfolio changes are an attempt to move away from total reliance on fixed income assets to secure some capital growth and provide a hedge against inflation. The Lawrences can afford to be somewhat aggressive with their IRAs because of the good pension and Social Security benefits they'll receive when Fred retires.

Fred should open up a self-directed IRA and transfer his high-yield fund to it. Next, he should cash in the first CD when it comes due and add a balanced fund to his holdings to participate in growth in the equity markets. He should use the proceeds from the second CD to purchase a conservative real estate investment trust for current yield and a chance at capital appreciation. This should help him keep up with inflation. He shouldn't follow the neighbor's suggestion on the limited partnership, because this is too illiquid for someone at his stage in life. He might also want to consider taking the cash from the third CD and investing it in income shares in a dual purpose fund with a relatively good current yield and a chance for dividend growth.

Now that Sally's spousal IRA has built up to $2,000, it could be invested in a medium-term bond fund or some five-year zero coupon bonds to generate higher yields along with some protection of principal. If all the above recommendations are followed, the Lawrences' IRA portfolios would look like this, assuming the balanced fund is counted as invested one-half in stocks and the other half in bonds:

Recommended Portfolio Mix for
Fred and Sally Lawrence

	Percent Invested			
	Original		*Reposition*	
Fixed Income				
Short-term	81		11	
Long-term	19		19	
Total		100		30
Equities		0		46
Real Estate		0		24
Total		100		100

The Lawrence IRA picture changes from one of being 100% in fixed income assets to being more evenly split between fixed income and equities, although these would be considered conservative equity positions. Further diversification is provided by the real estate investment.

Retiree and Spouse

Jack and Dorothy Slater are a retired couple living on Hilton Head Island, South Carolina. Jack, who recently quit work for the last time, is 68 and Dorothy is four years younger. Jack gets a medium-size pension of $25,000 from one of his former employers. This, plus his Social Security and life savings, are adequate for the both of them to live comfortably on. They own their house mortgage-free and real estate taxes are very low in this retirement community.

However, the Slaters are concerned with the impact inflation, particularly the double digit kind, will have on their future living costs. Jack's pension is not adjusted upwards for changes in the consumer price index. He and Dorothy are both worried about the Social Security System and whether those benefits will continue to keep pace with inflation. They would also like to leave a large estate to their two daughters and feel the tax-deferred capital build-up in the IRA will be a big help in achieving this goal.

The Slaters were fairly conservative with their investments until recently, when Jack opened an account with a discount broker. He enjoys playing the market now that he has the time to study its movements and follow individual stocks. A voracious reader of investment literature, Jack particularly likes buying out-of-favor stocks. The Slaters have $75,000 in equity investments which earn them an additional $4,000 a year in dividends. Their total annual income is about $40,000, of which $10,000 is plowed back into the stock portfolio.

As far as the IRA funds are concerned, for the most part they're also invested in stocks. In addition to his own IRA contributions and the spousal IRA he set up for Dorothy in 1982, Jack rolled over $45,000 from a qualified pension plan into his IRA. He made his last IRA contribution in 1985, the year he stopped working.

Jack has a self-directed IRA with his discount brokerage firm, which is now worth about $76,000. He has dividends swept into a money market fund within the IRA, and then uses these funds to make new investments. At any one time he usually has a small portfolio of about eight to ten stocks. Jack will be forced to make mandatory withdrawals from his IRA in two years when he reaches 70 and 1/2.

The following is the Slater's IRA portfolio:

Current IRAs of Jack and Dorothy Slater

Type and name	*Date Purchaed*	*Cost*	*Current Value*	*Current Yield*
Fixed Income				
Money Market Fund (Jack)	Various	$ 2,500	$ 3,000	9.5
Money Market Fund (Dorothy)	Various	750	1,000	9.5
Equities				
Common Stocks (Jack)	Various	51,000	$75,000	6.5%
Total		$54,250	$78,000	

Jack has been a fairly conservative investor with regard to his IRA stocks. Because their betas are low, they don't fluctuate as much as the rest of the market. Over 60% of his holdings are in utility and telephone company stocks that pay good dividends and also offer a chance for some appreciation. He also has what he considers to be undervalued capital goods and smokestack company stocks. Jack has held his own in the stock market, as can be seen from the numbers above. Although it appears as though his investments have gone up by 50%, when you figure the return on an annual compound basis, it works out to close to 10% a year.

Jack should consider diversifying his stock portfolio into areas that provide more protection against inflation. The telephone company stocks offer some of this, but the electric utility stocks don't because they often have a hard time increasing rates in the face of increasing costs. A portion of Jack's funds, probably 15%, should go into real estate investment trusts that pay good dividends and provide a hedge against inflation.

Part of Jack's portfolio is also very interest rate sensitive. That is, if interest rates ratchet upwards, the value of his portfolio will move in the opposite direction. High-yielding stocks such as utility shares often fall into this category. In order to insulate himself from sudden changes in Federal Reserve policy, Jack might consider putting some equity funds into more growth-oriented situations. An alternative might be to write options on his stock portfolio to gain additional income. He certainly has the time to spend and the right size portfolio to experiment with this investing technique.

Jack has done very well maintaining liquidity in his IRA so that when it comes time for mandatory withdrawals, he'll have no trouble cashing in his stocks to meet the payments. Since he's in relatively good financial shape, he will undoubtedly want to withdraw funds slowly using the IRS joint life expectancy tables and adjusting each year the minimum percentage to be withdrawn. This way, more funds will continue compounding in the IRA on a tax-deferred basis for him and Dorothy, and after their demise, some may be left over for their daughters.

The Slater's recommended IRA portfolio, modified for the real estate investments, would otherwise not change very much except for varying the stock mix from the current heavy concentration in utilities toward more growth oriented situations.

Recommended Portfolio Mix for
Jack and Dorothy Slater

	Percent Invested			
	Original		*Reposition*	
Fixed Income				
Short-term	5		5	
Long-term	0		0	
Total		5		5
Equities		95		80
Real Estate		0		15
Total		100		100

Elderly Widow

Deborah Hunt, age 64, lives in Indianapolis, Indiana. Stephen, her husband of 42 years suddenly passed away last year and now she's faced with trying to exist on a small pension plus Social Security benefits. Steve had no insurance or other assets when he died. Debbie needs to use her IRA to live on and can't afford to lose any principal.

Both Debbie and Steve grew up in the Indianapolis area, raising their two boys in the same house where she now lives by herself. Steve worked in a variey of jobs until he settled on a career with the local newspaper. At the time of his death, he and Debbie were receiving a modest pension; this was reduced in half to $7,000 when Debbie started to collect it as the surviving spouse. Debbie's Social Security benefits of $5,000 a year gives her a total income of $12,000, barely enough to get by on.

She wants to stay in the house in which she's lived for 23 years. It has a small mortgage on it, which Debbie pays off at the rate of $137 a month. Property taxes, however, are a relatively high $1,200 a year. Debbie lives fairly close to her oldest son, who is a lawyer in Indianapolis. Her other son teaches in Columbus, Ohio. Although her sons have offered to help financially, she's a proud woman and doesn't want any support from them.

After Steve's death his IRA was rolled into Debbie's, which now totals $11,000. Debbie is considering adding to these funds by taking part-time baby sitting jobs in her neighborhood. She feels a bit lonely being at home by herself and would like the chance to get out of the house more often. Her sons agree it would be good for her to take some part-time work to get her mind off the loss of Steve.

Debbie thinks she could add $2,000 a year to her IRA for the next six years. Her sons advised that if she earned 10% on current IRA funds and the extra years' contributions, it would total about $28,000 by the time she reached 70 and 1/2 and began mandatory withdrawals. At that time she would be forced to take out almost $2,000 a year, which would be a good addition to her pension and Social Security benefits. Meanwhile, at a 10% return, the account balance would continue building for the first several years before it began to diminish as she approached 80.

Debbie's IRA is now invested in bank CDs maturing every year. The funds are about evenly split between two banks and are fully insured with the Federal Deposit Insurance Corporation. As they come due, however, it seems they're always rolled over into new CDs at lower and lower rates. Debbie is concerned that she won't be able to meet her goal of earning at least 10% on her IRA funds.

Clearly, Debbie wants to invest as conservatively as possible to preserve her principal. She needs to hold onto every IRA dollar at her disposal. At the moment, she has perfect security with the CDs. However, as she's discovered, their returns are subject to swings in short-term interest rates.

She should consider lengthening her CD maturites or opening a self-directed account and buying some medium-term zero coupon bonds. These pay higher interest rates and she needn't worry about

Current IRAs of Deborah Hunt

Type and name	Date Purchased	Cost	Current Value	Current Yield
Fixed Income				
CDs at Bank A	Various	$4,500	$ 5,500	9.8
CDs at Bank B	Various	4,500	5,550	10.0
Total		$9,000	$11,050	

reinvesting the interest payments, as this is done automatically for her through the accrued interest mechanism.

In addition, she should consider putting 10% of the IRA assets in a medium-term bond fund that also pays several percentage points more than the new CDs she'll be stuck with. Even though interest rates are down, she shouldn't be tempted to go for the highest yield available in the long-term market. If interest rates rise again, then she will be locked in at lower rates or face a loss of principal.

Debbie's revised IRA portfolio will look like this:

Recommended Portfolio Mix for Deborah Hunt

	Percent Invested			
	Original		Reposition	
Fixed Income				
Short-term	100		50	
Medium-term	0		50	
Total		100		100
Equities		0		0
Real Estate		0		0
Total		100		100

Basically, Debbie has gone out on the yield curve in search of higher returns, but at the same time she's not subjecting herself to wide fluctuations in the long-term bond markets. She now has the best of both worlds.

******

A series of interesting case studies have been presented covering a variety of persons in varying circumstances. As is evident, a lot of portfolio switching is not necessary to bring IRA investments in line with a person's goals and objectives. Often it's just a matter of fine tuning. With proper attention, you and your advisors should be able to devise an investment program that maximizes the potential of your self-directed IRA and results in steady growth of your retirement nest egg.

APPENDIX A
List of Limited Partnerships Suitable for IRAs

Following are some limited partnerships that may be considered for IRAs. These are not recommendations, but were selected on the basis of the experience of the general partner and the number of prior public progams managed. A variety of partnership types are listed to provide a broad range of investment choices. Readers should check with their broker or financial planner for information on additional partnerships that may be suitable for self-directed IRAs.

One further note: many sponsors of limited partnerships will offer one partnership immediately followed by another after the first has been sold out. Both partnerships will have the same name but different numerical designations (e.g., August Income Properties I, August Income Properties II, etc.). However, the basic characteristics of each offering usually don't change from program to program.

Medium-Leverage Real Estate

These limited partnerships provide some leverage for those interested in having more than just their IRA contributions working for them. The early year tax benefits of leveraged partnerships are lost to IRA investors, and this must be taken into consideration. In addition, don't expect to receive any cash distributions for a few years. However, higher than normal capital gains could be down the road if the properties eventually appreciate in value.

Name	*Sponsor*	*Min. Inv.*	*Leverage*	*Type*
Angeles Income Properties	Angeles/Quinoco Corp. 10301 W. Pico Blvd. Los Angeles, CA 90064 800-421-4373	$2000	45%	Existing Comm. & Res.
August Properties Fund	August Financial Partners 3545 Long Beach Blvd. Long Beach, CA 90807 800-821-3320	2000	50	Existing Comm. & Res.
Balcor Current Income Fund	Balcor/American Express 4849 Golf Rd. Skokie, IL 60067 312-677-2900	2000	50	Existing Comm. & Res.
Centennial Development Fund	Centennial Group 282 S. Anita Dr. Orange, CA 92680 714-634-9200	2000	65	Land Dev.
Dain Pension Investors	Dain Bosworth 1820 Dain Tower Minneapolis, MN 55402 612-371-7810	2000	40	Existing Comm. & Res.
Equitec Real Estate Investors Fund	Equitec Financial Group 7677 Oakport St. Oakland, CA 94614 415-430-9900	2000	35	Existing Comm.
Hutton/Con Am Realty Investors	E.F. Hutton 1225 Franklin Ave. Garden City, NY 11530 516-747-8000	2000	50	Existing Res.
JMB Income Properties	JMB Realty Corp. 875 N. Michigan Ave. Chicago, IL 60611 800-621-1870	2000	35	Existing Comm.

(*continued*)

Name	Sponsor	Min. Inv.	Leverage	Type
USAA Income Properties	USAA Financial Services 9800 Fredericksburg Rd. San Antonio, TX 78288 800-531-8181	2000	45	Existing Comm. & Res.

Unleveraged Real Estate

These programs either do not use leverage or employ only a small amount of leverage to finance the purchase of properties. They will not have the upside capital appreciation potential of the leveraged real estate programs, but a lesser amount of tax benefits are lost. With unleveraged programs, IRA investors get current cash distributions. Some sponsors attempt to refinance their properties after a certain number of years to return capital to investors.

Name	Sponsor	Min. Inv.	Type
Balcor Equity Pension Inv.	Balcor/American Express 4849 Golf St. Skokie, IL 60077 312-677-2900	1000	Existing Comm/ Res. and Partic. Mtge.
Commercial Development Fund	Shearson/American Express 2 World Trade Center New York, NY 10048 212-321-6788	2000	New Comm.
Connecticut General Equity Partners	Connecticut General 950 Cottage Grove Rd. Bloomfield, CT 06152 203-726-3505	2000	Existing Comm.
High Equity Partners	Integrated Resources 666 3rd Ave. New York, NY 10017 800-223-1424	1000	Existing Comm.
I.R.E. Pension Investors	IRE Financial Services 2000 S. Dixie Highway Miami, FL 33133 305-858-6750	2000	Existing Comm.

(continued)

Name	Sponsor	Min. Inv.	Type
MLH Income Realty Partnership	Merrill Lynch 25 Broadway New York, NY 10004 212-709-4637	2000	Existing Comm. & Res.
Murray Income Properties	Murray Realty Inv. 5520 LBJ Freeway Dallas, TX 75240 214-851-6600	2000	New Comm.
NTS Properties	NTS Development Co. 10170 Linn Station Rd. Louisville, KY 40223 502-426-4800	2000	Comm. & Res. Dev.
National Real Estate Income Properties	National Development and Investment, Inc. 13555 Bishop Ct. Brookfield, WI 53005 800-558-1312	2000	Existing Comm. & Res.
New England Life Pension Prop.	New England Life 635 Boylston St. Boston, MA 02116 800-343-7104	2000	Existing/New Const.
Nooney Income Fund	Nooney Investors 7701 Forsyth Blvd. St. Louis, MO 63105 800-325-0893	2000	Existing Comm.
Paine Webber Equity Partners	Paine Webber Prop. 100 Federal St. Boston, MA 02101 617-423-8150	2000	Existing Comm. & Res.
Prudential Acquisition Fund	Prudential-Bache 100 Gold St. New York, NY 10292 212-791-1000	1000	Existing Comm.
Public Storage Properties	Public Storage 990 S. Fair Oaks Ave. Pasedena, CA 91109 800-421-2856	2000	New Mini-warehouses
R.I.C. Ltd.	Realty Income Corp. 200 W. Grand Ave. Escondido, CA 800-854-1967	2000	Fast Food Franchise Buildings

(*continued*)

Name	*Sponsor*	*Min. Inv.*	*Type*
Sierra Pacific Pension Inv.	Sierra Pacific Capital Co. 3 Corporate Plaza Newport Beach, CA 92660 714-640-8960	2000	New Comm.
Shurguard Income Properties	Shurguard Inc. 999 Third Ave. Seattle, WA 98104 206-628-3200	2000	Existing Mini-warehouses
Southmark Equity Partners	Southmark Corp. 1601 LBJ Freeway Dallas, TX 75234 800-421-3757	1000	Existing Comm. & Res.
T. Rowe Price Realty Income Fund	T.Rowe Price 100 E. Pratt St. Baltimore, MD 800-638-5660	2000	Existing Comm.
USSA Real Estate Income Inv.	USSA Financial Svs. 9800 Fredericksburg Rd. San Antonio, TX 78288 800-531-8181	2000	Existing Comm/ Res. & 1st Mtg.

Mortgage Loans

These limited partnerships invest in various types of mortgages. They provide high current income, and in some cases a chance at participating in the cash flows and profits on sales of the underlying properties. The risk characteristics of each program depend on a variety of factors, including the type of mortgage and the loan to appraised value ratio.

Name	*Sponsor*	*Min. Inv.*	*Type*
American Insured Mortgage Inv.	Integrated Resources 666 Third Ave. New York, NY 10017 800-223-1424	1000	FHA Insured; 1/2 Partic.

(*continued*)

Name	Sponsor	Min. Inv.	Type
August Pension Investors	August Financial Partners 3545 Long Beach Blvd. Long Beach, CA 90807 800-821-3332	2000	Loans to Affiliates
Balcor Pension Investors	Balcor/American Express 4849 Golf Road Skokie, IL 60077 312-677-2900	1000	Partic. 1st, 2nd, & Wraps
ConCap Instit. Properties	Consolidated Capital 1900 Powell St. Emeryville, CA 94608 800-227-1870	1000	Loans to Affiliates
Equitec Mortgage Investors Fund	Equitec Financial Group 7677 Oakport St. Oakland, CA 94614 415-430-9900	2000	Partic. 1st and Wraps
Insured Pension Investors	E.F. Hutton 1225 Franklin Ave. Garden City, NY 11530 516-747-8000	2000	1st, Ground Lease
Jacques-Miller Income Fund	Jacques-Miller, Inc. 211 7th Ave., N. Nashville, TN 37219 800-251-2003	1000	Loans to Affiliates
JMB Mortgage Partners	JMB Realty Corp. 875 N. Michigan Ave. Chicago, IL 60611 800-621-1870	1500	Partic. 1st
Paine Webber Qualified Plan Porperty Fund	Paine Webber Properties 100 Federal St. Boston, MA 02101 617-423-8150	2000	Partic. Ground Lease
Resources Pension Shares	Integrated Resources 666 Third Ave. New York, NY 10017 800-223-1424	1000	Partic. Wrap, Land Sale Leaseback
VMS Mortgage Investors	VMS Realty, Inc. 8700 W. Bryn Mawr Ave. Chicago, IL 60631 312-399-8700	1000	Partic. Wrap, 1st, 2nd to affiliates

Oil and Gas Income Funds

The limited partnerships listed below engage in little or no borrowing, which as many investors have found out is a risky business if the price of oil or gas drops. Nor do any of the programs have any assessments which require the limited partners to make additional investments. Several of the programs are limited partnerships that are traded in the public markets. The last column indicates where the general partner will purchase oil and gas properties.

Name	*Sponsor*	*Min. Inv.*	*Location*
Apache Petroleum Depositary Shares*	Apache Corporation 1800 Foshay Towers Minneapolis, MN 55402 612-332-7222	Listed NYSE	Continental US and Offshore
Damson Instit. Oil and Gas Income Fund	Damson Oil Corp. 366 Madison Ave. New York, NY 10017 800-223-1460	2000	Continental US
Enex Oil and Gas Income Program*	Enex Resources Corp. 1 Kingswood Plaza Kingswood, TX 77339 800-231-0444	2000	Continental US
Merrico Oil and Gas Income Funds*	Merrico Resources Inc. 1000 Energy Center Ardmore, OK 73402 800-654-4597	2000	Continental US
Quinoco Pension Investors Oil and Gas Income Program*	Quinoco Oil and Gas 645 5th Ave. New York, NY 10022 212-308-1010	2000	Continental US
Snyder Oil Partners	Snyder Exploration 1360 Post Oak Blvd. Houston, TX 77056 713-932-8016	Listed NYSE	Continental US

* May borrow between 8% and 20%.

Equipment Leasing Income Funds

These limited partnerships do not borrow funds to finance the purchase of equipment. The benefits to IRA investors are early and high cash flows; however, there is little or no capital appreciation potential because the equipment is subject to wear and tear and obsolescence. In some cases, the general partner will use part of the cash flow in the first several years to purchase additional equipment.

Name	*Sponsor*	*Min. Inv.*	*Type*
IEA Income Fund	IEA Securities Corp. 540 Howard St. San Francisco, CA 94105 415-543-7363	2000	Cargo Containers
Equitec Venture Leasing Investors	Equitec Financial Group 7677 Oakport St. Oakland, CA 94614 415-430-9900	2000	Manufacturing
National Lease Income Fund	Integrated Resources 666 Third Ave. New York, NY 10017 800-223-1424	1000	Info Systems and Office Machines
Phoenix Leasing Income Fund	Phoenix Leasing P.O. Box 2008 San Raphael, CA 94912 800-227-2626	2000	Computer Peripherals
PLM Transportation Equipment Partners	PLM Financial Services 655 Montgomery St. San Francisco, CA 94111 800-227-0830	2000	Transportation
Polaris Aircraft Income Fund	Polaris Securities 600 Montgomery St. San Francisco, CA 9411 800-227-3530	2000	Comm.and Business airplanes

APPENDIX B
List of Mutual Funds Suitable for IRAs

Following are some mutual funds that may be considered for IRAs, depending on the individual investor's goals and objectives and willingness to assume risk. Most of them are no-load funds with above-average performance for their respective fund category over recent five and ten-year periods. These are not necessarily recommendations, but merely a listing of a variety of funds which offer IRA programs, along with information on the minimum IRA investment required, whether or not the fund is part of a "family of funds," the size of the fund at September, 1985, and the year the fund began.

Readers should write the fund advisors for their most recent prospectuses and annual reports, and then discuss the suitability of purchasing them with their investment counselors.

Growth Funds

The objective of these funds is maximum capital gains through the purchase of common stocks of growth companies. Aggressive growth funds, as the name implies, invest in shares of smaller companies whose sales and earnings are expanding rapidly. These companies usually pay little or no dividends, but plow earnings back into working capital or capital investments. The stocks are fairly volatile compared to the market and so are the net asset values of the aggressive funds. Portfolio turnover is usually high because the fund advisors employ an active trading policy.

In general, growth funds are not quite as risky as the aggressive growth funds. Like their sister funds, they are only suitable IRA investments for persons who can afford to take capital losses in their accounts and are willing to invest for the long term. Many IRA investors will want to place a small percentage of their assets in these funds to add a growth element to their portfolios.

Name	*Advisor and Fund Address*	*Minimum and Subsequent IRA Investment*	*Family of Funds*	*Assets/ Year Began*
Fidelity Discoverer Fund	Fidelity Mgt. & Res. 82 Devonshire St. Boston, MA 02109 800-225-6190	$500 250	Yes	$123 mil. 1978
Janus Fund	Janus Mgt. Corp. 100 Filmore St. Denver, CO 80206 800-525-3713	None None	Yes	414 mil. 1961
Lehman Capital Fund	Lehman Mgt. Co. 55 Water St. New York, NY 10041 800-221-5350	250 100	Yes	123 mil. 1976
Stein Roe Special Fund	Stein Roe & Farnham 150 S. Wacker Dr. Chicago, IL 60606 800-621-7826	500 50	Yes	269 mil. 1968
Tudor Fund	Tudor Mgt. Co. One New York Plaza New York, NY 10004 800-223-3332	1000 50	No	139 mil. 1968

(*continued*)

Name	Advisor and Fund Address	Minimum and Subsequent IRA Investment	Family of Funds	Assets/ Year Began
Weingarten Equity Fund	Weingarten Mgt. Corp. 331 Madison Ave. New York, NY 10017 212-557-8787	1000 100	No	149 mil. 1967

Growth-Income Funds

These funds put some emphasis on the generation of dividend income, but they're still heavily oriented toward capital gain. They provide the IRA investor with higher current income than the pure growth funds. Income dividends to shareholders are paid quarterly and capital gain dividends are paid annually.

Name	Advisor and Fund Address	Minimum and Subsequent IRA Investment	Family of Funds	Assets/ Year Began
Fidelity Fund	Fidelity Mgt. & Res. 82 Devonshire St. Boston, MA 02109 800-225-6190	$500 250	Yes	$703 mil. 1930
Guardian Mutual Fund	Neuberger and Berman 342 Madison Avenue New York, NY 10173 800-367-0770	250 50	Yes	488 mil. 1965
Mutual Shares Corp.	Heine Securities 26 Broadway New York, NY 10004 800-221-7864	None None	No	827 mil. 1949
Mutual Qualified Income	Heine Securities 26 Broadway New York, NY 10004 800-221-7864	1000 None	No	335 mil. 1980

(continued)

Name	Advisor and Fund Address	Minimum and Subsequent IRA Investment	Family of Funds	Assets/ Year Began
Rowe Price Growth and Income Fund	T. Rowe Price 100 E. Pratt Street Baltimore, MD 21202 800-638-5660	500 100	Yes	347 mil. 1983
Strong Total Return Fund	Strong/Corneliuson Capital Management 815 E. Mason Street Milwaukee, WI 53202 800-368-3863	250 200	No	192 mil. 1982
Vanguard Trustees' Commingled-U.S. Portfolio	Batterymarch Fin. Mgt. Vanguard Group Vanguard Financial Ctr. Valley Forge, PA 19482 800-523-7025	500 100	Yes	207 mil. 1980
Wellesley Income Fund	Wellington Mgt. Co. Vanguard Group Vanguard Financial Ctr. Valley Forge, PA 19482 800-523-7025	500 100	Yes	160 mil. 1970
Windsor Fund II	Wellington Mgt. Co. Vanguard Group Vanguard Financial Ctr. Valley Forge, PA 19482 800-523-7025	500 100	Yes	138 mil. 1984

Income Funds

Income funds can be sub-categorized into equity-income funds and balanced funds. Equity-income funds are a type that are excellent choices for IRAs. The fund managers emphasize high dividend paying common stocks, so IRA investors can hope for relatively large current returns and some growth in principal. Income dividends are paid on a quarterly basis. Balanced funds invest about half their assets in growth stocks and the other half in fixed-income securities. Their objective is to provide stable growth with relatively high yields.

Name	Advisor and Fund Address	Minimum and Subsequent IRA Investment	Family of Funds	Assets/ Year Began
Evergreen Total Return Fund	Saxon Woods Asset Management Corp. 550 Mamaroneck Ave. Harrison, NY 10528 914-698-5711	$1500 None	No	$144 mil. 1978
Fidelity Puritan Fund	Fidelity Mgt. & Res. 82 Devonshire Road Boston, MA 02109 800-225-6190	500 250	Yes	1075 mil. 1946
Financial Industrial Income Fund	Financial Programs P.O. Box 2040 Denver, CO 80201 800-525-9831	None None	Yes	353 mil. 1960
SAFECO Income Fund	SAFECO Asset Mgt. SAFECO Plaza Seattle, WA 98185 800-426-6730	250 100	Yes	31 mil. 1969
Selected American Shares	Vincent, Chesley Advisors 230 West Monroe St. Chicago, IL 60606 800-621-7321	1000 100	No	105 mil. 1933
Strong Investment Fund	Strong/Corneliuson Capital Mgt. 815 E. Mason St. Milwaukee, WS 53202 800-368-3863	250 200	No	203 mil. 1981
Value Line Income Fund	Value Line, Inc. 711 Third Ave. New York, NY 10017 800-223-0818	250 25	Yes	127 mil. 1952
Wellington Fund	Wellington Mgt. Co. Vanguard Group Vanguard Financial Ctr. Valley Forge, PA 19482 800-523-7025	500 100	Yes	723 mil. 1928

Bond Funds

Pure fixed-income funds offer the highest income yield, but may be somewhat volatile depending on the average length of maturity and the quality of the portfolio's bonds. The shorter the maturity, the less volatility of net asset value of the fund. There is little chance of long-term capital appreciation unless the trend of interest rates is down. Before investing, it is important to check the prospectus for the type of bonds bought by the fund's advisors, their quality ratings and their average length to maturity.

Name	*Advisor and Fund Address*	*Minimum and Subsequent IRA Investment*	*Family of Funds*	*Assets/ Year Began*
Dreyfus A Bond Plus	Dreyfus Corp. 600 Madison Ave. New York, NY 10022 800-645-6561	750 100	Yes	$156 mil. 1976
Fidelity High Income Fund	Fidelity Mgt. & Res. 82 Devonshire St. Boston, MA 02109 800-225-6190	500 250	Yes	591 mil. 1977
Fidelity Thrift Trust	Fidelity Mgt. & Res. 82 Devonshire St. Boston, MA 02109 800-225-6190	500 250	Yes	210 mil. 1975
Northeast Investors Trust	Northeast Investors Trust 50 Congress St. Boston, MA 02109 800-225-6704	500 None	No	214 mil. 1950
T. Rowe Price New Income Fund	T. Rowe Price Assoc. 100 E. Pratt St. Baltimore, MD 21202 800-638-5660	500 100	Yes	792 mil. 1973
Scudder Income Fund	Scudder, Stevens & Clark 175 Federal St. Boston, MA 02110 800-225-2470	240 None	Yes	152 mil. 1928
Southwestern Investors Income Fund	Tenneco Asset Mgt. Co. 777 Walker Ave. Houston, TX 77002 800-231-0808	None None	No	11 mil. 1968
USAA Income	USAA Investment Mgt. 9800 Fredericksburg Rd. San Antonio, TX 78288 800-531-8181	250 25	Yes	134 mil. 1973

(*continued*)

Name	Advisor and Fund Address	Minimum and Subsequent IRA Investment	Family of Funds	Assets/ Year Began
Vanguard High-Yield Bond Portfolio	Wellington Mgt. Co. Vanguard Financial Ctr. Valley Forge, PA 19482 800-523-7025	500 100	Yes	392 mil. 1978

International Funds

These mutual funds invest a majority of their assets in stocks of companies domiciled in foreign countries. They provide IRA owners with a degree of diversification away from the United States markets. The international stock markets often move in the opposite direction of the American markets, so these funds also serve as a hedge against a downturn in the domestic stock market.

Name	Advisor and Fund Address	Minimum and Subsequent IRA Investment	Family of Funds	Assets/ Year Began
G. T. Pacific Fund	G. T. Capital Mgt. 601 Montgomery St. San Francisco, CA 94111 800-824-1580	500 100	No	$43 mil. 1977
Ivest Fund	Vanguard Group Vanguard Financial Ctr. Valley Forge, PA 19482 800-523-7025	500 100	Yes	191 mil. 1961
Rowe Price International Fund	Rowe Price-Fleming International 100 E. Pratt St. Baltimore, MD 21202 800-638-5660	500 100	Yes	249 mil. 1980
Scudder International Fund	Scudder, Stevens & Clark 175 Federal St. Boston, MA 02110 800-225-2470	1000 None	Yes	303 mil. 1953

(*continued*)

Name	Advisor and Fund Address	Minimum and Subsequent IRA Investment	Family of Funds	Assets/ Year Began
Transatlantic Fund, Inc.	Kleinwort Benson 100 Wall Street New York, NY 10005 212-747-0040	1000 500	No	28 mil. 1959

Convertible Bond Funds

These funds invest a majority of shareholder assets in convertible preferred stocks and convertible bonds. The objective is to generated current income with a chance for capital gain if the shares of the underlying stocks increase in value. Some protection against declining share prices is provided by the floor on the price of the bonds when they trade as equivalent straight debt securities. Because of these characteristics, convertible bond funds are particularly suitable for IRAs.

Name	Advisor and Fund Address	Minimum and Subsequent IRA Investment	Family of Funds	Assets/ Year Began
Bancroft Convertible Fund	Davis/Dinsmore Mgt. 42 Broadway New York, NY 10004 212-269-9236	Closed end	No	46 mil. 1971
Castle Convertible Fund	Fred Alger Mgt. 75 Maiden Lane New York, NY 10038 212-806-8800	Closed end	No	33 mil. 1971
Convertible Yield Securities (load)	AIM Advisors 11 Greenway Plaza Houston, TX 77046 800-231-0803	$500 100	No	21 mil. 1978

(*continued*)

Name	Advisor and Fund Address	Minimum and Subsequent IRA Investment	Family of Funds	Assets/ Year Began
Noddings-Calamos Convertible Income and Growth Funds	Noddings-Calamos & Associates 2002 Spring Road Oakbook, IL 60521 800-251-2411	2000 100	No	3 mil. 1985
Phoenix Convertible Fund Series (load)	Phoenix Investment Counsel One American Row Hartford, CT 06115 203-278-8050	500 50	Yes	63 mil. 1972
Putnam Convertible Fund (load)	Putnam Mgt. Co. One Post Office Sq. Boston, MA 02109 617-292-1000	500 50	Yes	61 mil. 1972
Value Line Convertible Bond Fund	Value Line, Inc. 711 Third Ave. New York, NY 10017 800-223-0818	1000 250	Yes	23 mil. 1985

Appendix C
IRA Questions and Answers

Contributions

Q. Under tax reform, exactly who is eligible to make an IRA contribution?

A. Anyone who has earned income can make a contribution to an IRA. However, as explained below, only certain persons can deduct the contribution from adjusted gross income.

Q. Why should I make a contribution if I can't deduct it?

A. You can still get the advantage of tax-deferred buildup of earnings on your funds inside the IRA. This is a faster way of building a retirement nest egg than investing outside the IRA and paying taxes on the earnings. This is especially true when capital gain income is taxed at the same rates as ordinary income.

Q. What is the deadline for establishing and contributing to an IRA for a tax deduction?

A. Your IRA must be set up and funded by April 15th of the year following the year for which the contribution is made. You no longer can contributed beyond this date, even if you're granted an extension for filing your income tax returns.

Q. Is there a "best" time for me to contribute each year? Should I contribute all at once or make payments on an installment basis?
A. The earlier you get your IRA fully funded for the year, the sooner earnings on your contributions will begin compounding tax-deferred. Naturally, this means that a lump sum contributed at the beginning of the year has more earning potential than either one made later in the year or a series of small contributions made throughout the year. Persons who only want to contribute if they can take the deduction may have a problem determining what their adjusted gross income will be at the beginning of the year. They may want to wait until they can determine whether they qualify for a deduction before making the contribution.

Q. Do I need to work a certain number of hours annually to establish an IRA?
A. No. Anyone who is employed and earning income is eligible to make the contribution. Divorced persons receiving alimony are also eligible. You can contribute an amount equal to your earnings or alimony, up to $2,000, or $2,250 if one spouse is not working. However, as explained below, only certain persons may deduct the contribution from adjusted gross income.

Q. Are there any minimum age requirements? Do I need to be of legal age?
A. There is no minimum age requirement. You can established an IRA as early in your employment career as you like, even if you're under legal age.

Q. Are there any maximum age requirements for IRA contributions?
A. Yes, you cannot set up an IRA or contribute to it after the last year in which you turn 70 and 1/2. For example, if your 70th birthday is in July of 1986, you can contribute to an IRA until December 31, 1987 as long as you're still working and earning income. After that date, you cannot contribute to your own account and must begin to withdraw funds. However, if you work, you can still contribute to your spouse's account until he or she reaches 70 and 1/2.

Q. Is there a minimum annual contribution requirement?

A. No. You are permitted to contribute as little as you choose in any year. In fact, you aren't even required to make payments in any year if you don't want to add to an existing account. However, some IRA plans require a minimum initial contribution and minimum additional investment requirements for participation.

Q. Is there a maximum contribution limit?
A. You can contribute no more than $2,000 in a year to any one IRA.

Q. Must all contributions be made in cash?
A. Yes. Cash, checks, or money orders are acceptable. Rollovers from qualified retirement plans may be made in cash or securities and rollovers from other IRAs must be in cash. IRA transfers from one account to another may be with securities.

Q. Am I limited to having only one IRA? If not, how many can I have?
A. You can have as many IRAs as you wish, but you cannot make a combined total contribution exceeding $2,000 in any year. Also, remember that too many annual maintenance fees for separate accounts could be expensive. If diversification is your goal, there are investments available, such as mutual funds, that already have this feature built in.
(*Note:* New tax law changes may require separate accounts for deductible and nondeductible IRA contributions.)

Q. Can I contribute to an IRA from my savings and still take a deduction from my income at tax time?
A. Yes. But only if you're eligible for the deduction and your contribution is at least equal to your earned income in the year it was made.

Q. Is there any type of unearned income that I can include in the maximum contribution?
A. Absolutely not. With the exception of alimony received, only earned income counts. This means that gifts, capital gains, sweepstakes, inheritances, prizes, and gambling winnings don't count. Uncle Sam may be willing to let you shelter your hard-earned wages, salary, and self-employed income in an IRA, but he's reluctant to let you get away with sheltering other income.

Q. What about disability benefits? Do they count?
A. These benefits don't count either, because they're not considered earned income.

Q. I work for a foreign corporation and do not pay U.S. income tax on my earnings. Can I still contribute to an IRA?
A. Unfortunately not. The rule of thumb is that you can only contribute earnings upon which you would normally pay federal income tax. This excludes foreign sources of income.

Q. Can I contribute borrowed money to my IRA if I'm eligible, but do not have the cash on hand?
A. Yes, you can. But you can't deduct your interest expense for the loan on schedule A of your Form 1040. Tax reform has eliminated most interest deduction, and this is one of them.

Q. My spouse and I are a two-income couple and we file jointly. Do we establish a joint IRA?
A. No. There is no such thing as a joint IRA. Remember what IRA stands for: Individual Retirement Account. In your case, whether you file singly or jointly, you both are eligible to establish your own IRAs, each with a $2,000 per year limit.

Q. Can I contribute to an IRA for my nonworking spouse?
A. You can open a "spousal IRA" in addition to your own. You can contribute up to a total of $2,250 to both accounts, divided any way you choose between each account as long as no more than $2,000 goes into either.

Q. What kind of restrictions apply to spousal account contributions?
A. You can contribute to your nonworking spouse's account until he or she turns 70 and 1/2, even though you've already reached that age and can no longer contribute to your own account. Remember, $2,250 is the maximum annual contribution allowable to both accounts combined, and you must have enough earned income to support it.

Q. If I have established a spousal account in addition to my own account, must I contribute to both each year, or can I put money into only one if it suits my needs?
A. As long as you don't go over the $2,000 limit for one account, you can contribute solely to either account in any year.

Q. If we have a spousal account and my spouse begins to earn income, what happens to the account?
A. You can neither contribute to nor claim as a deduction a spousal IRA in any tax year during which your spouse is employed. Em-

ployed spouses are eligible to establish their own accounts into which they can transfer the funds from their spousal IRA

Q. Can I have IRA contributions automatically deducted from my checking account?
A. Yes. Many banks and mutual funds offer this service for IRA accounts.

Q. Can I arrange for my employer to contribute regular deductions from my paycheck to my IRA?
A. Yes. This is a very convenient way to fund your account. However, much of your total contribution will occur in the middle and latter part of the year and won't provide as fast a tax-deferred buildup of earnings as a large single contribution made at the beginning of the year. Your employer may also make the payments on your behalf and claim them as deductions on the corporate return. However, in this case, you wouldn't be able to take the deduction on your own tax return.

Q. Can I over- or under-contribute in one year to make up for an under- or over-contribution in another year?
A. There's a 6 percent penalty on an over-contribution in any year. An under-contribution cannot make you eligible to contribute more than $2,000 in another year. Nor does it excuse you from penalties incurred in prior years for an excess contribution.

Rollovers and Withdrawals

Q. What happens if I withdraw funds from my IRA before I reach age 59 and 1/2?
A. If these funds are not rolled over into another IRA, they will be subject to a 10 percent penalty on the amount of funds withdrawn, plus any taxes that are due. The only exception to the penalty is if the money is withdrawn in equal installments over a lifetime—through an annuity, for example.

Q. Will withdrawals from nondeductible IRA contributions be subject to the 10 percent penalty tax if the withdrawals take place before the owner reaches age 59 and 1/2?

A. No, the penalty will not apply to those funds, but will cover any earnings that build up on a tax-deferred basis.

Q. Is there any difference between transfers and rollovers of IRA funds?
A. Yes, there is. A transfer occurs when your funds are moved from one IRA plan to another by the trustee or custodian at your direction. It is a direct transaction, and you can do as many transfers as you want in any year. A rollover occurs when you take funds out of one IRA or another pension program, such as a Keogh or a profit sharing plan, and put the funds into another IRA. The same funds can only be rolled over once per calendar year. The rollover must be accomplished within 60 days to avoid penalties and taxes.

Q. Can I roll over a portion of my qualified retirement fund account into an IRA and keep the rest for my own use?
A. There's no reason why you can't do this if you wish. Remember that the amount rolled over will eventually be taxed along with other IRA distributions. The portion of retirement funds received directly in full or partial lump sum distributions is eligible for special five-year averaging at favorable tax rates, as long as it's all received within one year.

Q. Can I roll over funds received in a partial distribution from my qualified retirement plan into my IRA?
A. Under certain conditions, this may be done even if you continue to work for the same employer. The partial distribution cannot be a series of periodic distributions and must be equal to 50 percent of your retirement fund account balance. Furthermore, you must be eligible to take your money out. You might want to consider taking a partial distribution if the retirement plan's performance has been poor.

Q. Can I roll over all funds from a qualified plan into an IRA and then to another qualified plan?
A. Yes, but they must be rolled into a separate "conduit" IRA, where no mixing of retirement funds is allowed with an existing IRA. They can be held there until you are eligible to participate in another pension plan.

Q. What part of my qualified plan may I roll over?

A. That portion which comes from your contributions and earnings on these funds that haven't been taxed. Any voluntary contributions already taxed cannot be rolled over. Retirement plans which qualify include deferred profit sharing, defined benefit, ESOP, and employer mandatory contributions to thrift plans.

Q. Can I roll back my rollover?
A. Yes. If you start a rollover, then decide to return the funds to the original IRA, you can do this without penalty if it's done within 60 days. However, this counts as a rollover, so you can't touch those funds for at least a year.

Taxes

Q. Under tax reform, who is eligible to deduct IRA contributions from their income?
A. All wage earners whose income is less than $40,000 in the case of married persons, and $25,000 for single persons, will be allowed to deduct the full amount of their contribution up to $2,000 ($2,250 where only one spouse works). In addition, anyone who isn't covered by an employer's pension plan is eligible for the deduction, irrespective of how much he makes.

Q. If I haven't been in my job long enough to qualify for the company pension plan, am I then eligible for the IRA deduction?
A. Unfortunately not. You're considered a participant in a retirement plan whether or not your benefits are vested. Only those persons who have not met the plan's eligibility requirements (they're under the minimum wage or haven't worked at the employer long enough) can deduct the IRA contribution (as long as they remain outside the plan for the entire year).

Q. If my spouse and I have incomes of more than $50,000, but only one of us participates in an employee retirement plan, can we take the IRA deduction?
A. No. If one of you is covered, then neither can take the deduction.

Q. Aren't some persons allowed to take partial deductions?
A. Yes. Those couples who make between $40,000 and $50,000 will be able to take a pro-rata deduction that drops by $200 for every

$1,000 of their adjusted gross income above $40,000 (or $25,000 in the case of individuals). The exact amounts are listed below in hundreds of dollars:

	Earnings		
	Joint	*Single*	*IRA Deduction*
Up to:	$40,000	$25,000	$2,000
	41,000	26,000	1,800
	42,000	27,000	1,600
	43,000	28,000	1,400
	44,000	29,000	1,200
	45,000	30,000	1,000
	46,000	31,000	800
	47,000	32,000	600
	48,000	33,000	400
	49,000	34,000	200
Over:	50,000	35,000	0

For example, if a person earned $40,500, then he would be entitled to an IRA deduction of $1,900, which is halfway between the amounts allowed for those earning $40,000 and those earning $41,000. He could still contribute the full $2,000, but only $1,900 would be deductible from his adjusted gross income.

Q. Will an IRA further complicate my tax returns?
A. Accounting for your IRA at tax time is neither difficult nor complicated. Simply record the amount of your deductible contribution on the appropriate line of the Form 1040 where it says "adjustments to gross income." The only problem that could arise would be if you over-contributed or withdrew funds prematurely from your account, in which case you would need to fill out IRS FORM 5329, the Return for Individual Retirement Arrangement Taxes.

Q. Can I deduct contributions from my state and local income taxes?
A. In states and localities that have income taxes, an IRA usually gives you the same breaks as you get from federal taxes. You should contact your state and local tax offices for information on what deductions they allow and any penalties imposed for early withdrawals.

Q. Can I deduct capital losses on investments contained in my IRA?

A. No, because you already deducted the initial IRA contribution. You're not allowed double deductions in this case.

Q. May I adjust withholdings for my IRA contributions?
A. Yes, if you're eligible for the deduction. This will increase your take-home pay. For each $1,000 you've contributed, take an extra exemption on your W-4 form.

Q. How are IRA withdrawals reported to the IRS?
A. By January of each year the trustee or custodian of your IRA is required to give you and the IRS a statement of withdrawals or deemed distributions. For periodic payments, IRS Form W-2P is used. Nonperiodic payments such as one-time withdrawals will be reported on Form 1099R.

Q. How are IRA funds taxed once they're withdrawn from my account?
A. All funds that were contributed and deducted from adjusted gross incomes will be taxed when withdrawn. IRA funds that were contributed but not deducted won't be taxed when they're withdrawn. All earnings on IRA funds, including any capital gains, will be taxed on withdrawal.

Q. What if I have a mix of deductible and nondeductible contributions in my IRAs and I want to make a withdrawal? How is it then taxed?
A. Separate accounts will be needed to distinguish the two types of IRA funds. You will be allowed to withdraw the nondeductible contributions first and not pay taxes, but the tax-deferred earnings on the funds will be taxed on a pro-rata basis. For example, assume you had $12,000 in your nondeductible account, including $2,000 from earnings on the funds. If you withdrew $6,000, then $1,000 would be taxed and the balance would not be taxed.

Investments

Q. What alternative investments are available for my IRA?
A. Basically, there are four types of financial institutions offering IRA plans: (1) banks, credit unions, and savings and loans; (2) insurance companies; (3) mutual funds; and (4) brokerage firms. You can put your IRA funds in most of the same investment vehicles normally offered to non-IRA investors by each of these institutions.

Q. Are there are types of investments that I should generally avoid where my IRA is concerned?
A. You shouldn't invest your IRA funds in tax-exempt investments, like municipal bonds, because any IRA earnings are already sheltered from taxes. It doesn't make sense to accept the low yields such investments generate, especially when you consider that the funds will eventually be taxed as ordinary income upon withdrawal.

Q. What types of assets can't I purchase with my IRA funds?
A. Generally speaking, you're not allowed to invest in "collectibles" such as antiques or artwork, or pay life insurance premiums with IRA monies. The only exception is gold and silver coins issued by the United States government. Also, although the IRS permits it, you usually cannot make very speculative investments such as in commodities futures. Most brokerage firms will not allow IRA customers to purchase them because they regard the risk as too high.

Q. Can I purchase real estate with my IRA?
A. Although the direct purchase of real estate is allowed, it is not a common investment due to the $2,000 annual contribution ceiling, which limits your purchasing power until such time as you build up a sizable account. However, there are some real estate partnerships that accommodate small IRAs. Because they're unleveraged, they're designed to produce current income and hopefully capital appreciation when the property portfolio is eventually sold.

Q. May I own options or warrants in my IRA account?
A. Yes, although these are risky securities. Some brokerage houses do not permit these investments in customers' self-directed IRA accounts. A less speculative venture is to write puts and calls on stocks you hold in your IRA to generate extra income.

Q. If I have my IRA funds in a time investment, like a three-month certificate of deposit, can I begin withdrawals as soon as I am eligible or do I need to abide by the maturity date of my CD?
A. Although the IRS regulations are the legal standard, many banking institutions additionally stipulate that your investment must mature before you can begin to receive distributions. Otherwise, you'll lose your interest earnings. Some banks waive this restriction in the case of those IRA owners who reach age 59 and 1/2.

Q. Can I switch funds between IRA trustees and custodians?

A. You can transfer funds or securities directly from one IRA trustee/custodian to another as many times as you wish. However, you're allowed to "roll over" your funds only once a year. This means that you can take possession of the funds yourself, without penalty, for up to 60 days once each year before redepositing them with another custodian. But be careful to notify the original trustee that you intend to roll the funds over and don't want the 10 percent penalty withheld. Otherwise, the trustee may turn 10 percent over to the IRS and you'll have to claim it as a tax prepayment.

Q. Can I use my IRA as collateral for a loan?
A. Absolutely not. The IRS considers this to be an early withdrawal, which results in the imposition of the 10 percent penalty and ordinary income tax liability on the amount used as security for a loan.

Q. Can I have a margin account with my IRA?
A. No, because pledging IRA assets to borrow money is prohibited, and a margin call could put you over the $2,000 annual contribution limit.

Q. Is my IRA protected from creditors?
A. In a few states, such as California, it is. In most states, however, the IRA funds are not because they're considered part of your total assets.

Distributions

Q. At what age may I begin to receive distributions?
A. You can receive distributions at any time, but as soon as you turn 59 and 1/2, you can begin to withdraw funds from your IRA without penalty. Between ages 59 and 1/2 and 70 and 1/2 you can take out as little or as much as you like. Once you turn 70 and 1/2, though, you must make annual minimum withdrawals in accordance with IRS tables for your life expectancy, or joint life expectancy with either your spouse or some other person, whichever you choose.

Q. How does the calculation work?
A. You figure out your life expectancy, based on the IRS tables. For example, a single man, aged 70, is expected to live another 12 years, or until age 82 (for a woman the same age, it's 15 years). He would be required to withdraw at least 1/12th of the value of his IRA money the

first year, 1/11th of the remaining balance the second year, and so on until the funds in the account are completely withdrawn by the 12th year.

Q. Is there any other way to stretch this time period out longer?
A. Yes, using IRS tables you can recalculate your life expectancy in each subsequent year after you turn age 70 and 1/2. This will prevent you from outliving your distributions: the longer you actually live, the more you're expected to live longer. For example, if a 70 and 1/2 year old male lives to 82 and 1/2, he would still be expected to live another 7 years, but would have no IRA to draw on if he hadn't recalculated his life expectancy each year.

Q. Are there any other options?
A. There's one more. You can have the distribution spread over the joint life expectancy of yourself and any other individual such as your spouse, child, or grandchild. This serves to minimize the amount withdrawn and maximize the tax-deferred compounding or earnings left in your IRA. However, at least 50 percent of the funds have to be distributed over the IRA account holder's life expectancy. And you can't refigure joint life expectancies each year for anyone other than a spouse.

Q. How do you figure joint life expectancy with your spouse?
A. Go to the IRS annuity tables, which show joint life expectancies. Read across for male and down for female, or vice versa, until you come to the proper pair of ages. Move into the chart to find the appropriate joint life expectancy for the two of you.

Q. Are there any simpler alternatives to all the arithmetic involved in calculating mandatory withdrawals at age 70 and 1/2?
A. Yes. The IRS allows you to purchase a lifetime annuity at age 70 and 1/2 that will satisfy minimum withdrawal requirements. However, life insurance annuity payments are usually lower than what you can earn elsewhere.

Q. What is the exact trigger date for mandatory withdrawals once I reach 70 and 1/2?
A. They must begin by April 1 of the year following the year in which you hit that age.

Q. What if I don't meet the minimum withdrawal requirements when I reach 70 and 1/2?

A. You pay a 50 percent penalty on the shortfall.

Q. Is there any situation in which I can withdraw funds without penalty before age 59 and 1/2?
A. Yes, there are two ways. If it is medically shown that you are disabled and cannot continue to work in any occupation for twelve months or longer, you're allowed to withdraw funds at any time without penalty. However, you're still taxed on your withdrawals (except for nondeductible contributions), but presumably you'll be in a low bracket during a disability. The other way is to take the withdrawal as a lifetime annuity.

Q. Are there any other penalties on withdrawals?
A. Yes. Tax reform has imposed a 15 percent penalty on excess distributions in a given year from IRAs and qualified retirement plans. No more than $112,500 can be withdrawn from both without a penalty.

Q. How are funds distributed from a spousal account?
A. Distributions are made on the basis of individual age and account value, no matter which spouse is the working partner. Each spousal account is subject to the same distribution requirements.

Q. If I get divorced, what happens to my IRA?
A. In general, IRAs are individually owned and neither spouse has any legal claim to the other's account in the event of a divorce or separation. Spousal accounts can be used voluntarily in a settlement and IRA funds may be transferred between parties. In some states, if a settlement is contested in court, an IRA can become part of it.

Q. Are withholding taxes applicable to IRAs?
A. Taxes will automatically be withheld from the distribution unless you choose otherwise. Generally, it will be withheld at a 10 percent rate on nonperiodic distributions.

Estate Matters

Q. When I die, what happens to my IRA?
A. If your beneficiary is your spouse and you die before making mandatory withdrawals, then he or she can continue the tax deferment by leaving the account in your name or rolling it into his or her

account. If it's left in your name, there's no penalty on withdrawals after you would have turned 59 and 1/2, had you lived to that age.

Q. What if my beneficiary is not my spouse?
A. He or she may elect to have assets paid out over his or her life expectancy. These payments must start within one year of your death; if not, then all funds must be withdrawn from the account within a five-year period and income taxes paid on the withdrawals each year. There is no penalty. If mandatory payments had already begun, they can continue to a beneficiary at that rate or a faster one.

Q. If I inherit an IRA, may I roll it over into my own IRA?
A. No, unless you are the surviving spouse.

Q. Are there restrictions on whom I can designate as beneficiary?
A. The IRS has no regulations concerning this matter. You may designate any one or more persons, or a trust, partnership, corporation, charitable organization, or even your estate as your beneficiary or beneficiaries. You might even have secondary beneficiaries as well.

Q. If I have more than one IRA, may I have more than one beneficiary?
A. Yes, you may have as many beneficiaries as you want.

Q. What if I don't have a beneficiary named?
A. Monies in your IRA will be distributed by the trustee or custodian in accordance with the terms of the IRA agreement. It may go to a deemed beneficiary—deemed to be a particular person or entity. Otherwise, it may go to your estate.

Q. Does an IRA beneficiary need to report distributions to the IRS?
A. If there are still funds in the account, the answer is yes. A beneficiary must file with the IRS each tax year until the IRA balance reaches zero.

Q. If I inherit an IRA, will I have to pay taxes on it?
A. Yes, you will pay ordinary income tax on it as it is withdrawn. The money retains the same character for income tax purposes.

Q. Can inherited distributions be rolled over into another IRA?
A. Generally not. Only the surviving spouse may roll them over into another IRA.

Q. Can monies from a decedent's IRA be used to pay his or her debts?
A. State laws vary, but generally, IRA funds can be attached to pay estate taxes, administrative expenses, and the decedent's other debts.

Q. When I die, how is my IRA treated for estate tax purposes?
A. It is fully included in your estate and taxed accordingly. Naturally, you'll have the estate tax exemption of $600,000 in 1987 and thereafter, so you'll need a sizable estate before your beneficiaries will feel the pinch of estate taxes.

APPENDIX D
The Magic of Compounding in an IRA

IRA Earnings With Annual $2,000 Contributions

Annual Yield:	*8%*	*10%*	*12%*	*14%*	*15%*
Initial Investment	2,000	2,000	2,000	2,000	2,000
After One Year	2,160	2,200	2,240	2,280	2,300
	4,493	4,620	4,749	4,879	4,945
	7,012	7,282	7,559	7,842	7,987
	9,733	10,210	10,706	11,220	11,485
	12,672	13,431	14,230	15,071	15,507
	15,846	16,974	18,178	19,461	20,134
	19,273	20,872	22,599	24,466	25,454
	22,975	25,159	27,551	30,171	31,572
	26,973	29,875	33,097	36,675	38,607

(*continued*)

Annual Yield:	*8%*	*10%*	*12%*	*14%*	*15%*
After Ten Years	31,291	35,062	39,309	44,089	46,699
	35,954	40,769	46,266	52,541	56,003
	40,991	47,045	54,058	62,177	66,704
	46,430	53,950	62,785	73,162	79,009
	52,304	61,545	72,559	85,685	93,161
	58,649	69,899	83,507	99,961	109,435
	65,500	79,089	95,767	116,235	128,150
	72,900	89,198	109,499	134,788	149,673
	80,893	100,318	124,879	155,938	174,424
	89,524	112,550	142,105	180,050	202,887
After Twenty Years	98,846	126,005	161,397	207,537	235,620
	108,914	140,805	183,005	238,872	273,263
	119,787	157,086	207,206	274,594	316,553
	131,530	174,995	234,310	315,317	366,336
	144,212	194,694	264,668	361,742	423,586
	157,909	216,364	298,668	414,665	489,424
	172,702	240,200	336,748	474,999	565,138
	188,678	266,420	379,398	543,778	652,208
	205,932	295,262	427,166	622,187	752,339
	224,566	326,988	480,665	711,574	867,490
After Thirty Years	244,692	361,887	540,585	813,474	999,914
	266,427	400,276	607,695	929,640	1,152,201
	289,901	442,503	682,859	1,062,070	1,327,331
	315,253	488,953	767,042	1,213,040	1,528,731
	342,634	540,049	861,327	1,385,145	1,760,340
	372,204	596,254	966,926	1,581,346	2,026,691
	404,141	658,079	1,085,197	1,805,014	2,332,995
	438,632	726,087	1,217,661	2,059,996	2,685,244
	475,882	800,896	1,366,020	2,350,676	3,090,331
	516,113	883,185	1,532,183	2,682,050	3,556,181
After Forty Years	559,562	973,704	1,718,285	3,059,817	4,091,908

Appendix E

Discount Brokerage Firms

Self-directed IRA owners can save commissions by using discount brokerage firms. The savings range from 50 percent to 90 percent of normal commissions depending on the size of the trade and the firm employed. But do not expect to receive any investment advice for your self-directed IRA; the discounters are strictly order takers. And you're not assigned an account representative. Whoever picks up the phone when you call executes your order.

Discount brokers began in the mid-1970s when fixed commissions were abolished by the New York Stock Exchange. Brokerage houses were then free to negotiate commissions with customers. At first it was the large institutions that received discounts. Then a few brokerage firms responded to the demand for lower commissions from individuals who did their own research and picked their own stocks. Almost 10 percent of all trades done by individual investors now are handled through discount brokers.

In the last few years a number of new discount brokerage firms have started operations. They specialize in stocks, bonds, and options. Some even purchase mutual funds for customers. They all handle self-directed IRAs, either through their own custodian or with outside trustees. Many of the discounters have regional offices and toll-free "800" numbers for information or taking orders.

It should be noted that if you're making a small trade—say for $1,000 to $1,500 worth of stock—you will not save very much by using a discount broker. Minimum commissions of between $30 and $35 per trade are common for small trades. However, for trades greater than $2,000, the savings are more significant. The table below illustrates expected savings by using a discount broker:

Trade Amount	*Full-Service Broker Commission*	*Discount Broker Commission*	*Savings*	*Per Cent Savings*
$ 1,000	$ 35	$35	$ 0	0.0%
1,500	42	35	7	16.7
2,000	67	35	32	47.8
3,000	85	35	50	58.9
4,000	100	35	65	65.0
5,000	115	38	77	67.0
10,000	200	65	135	67.5

Basic information on some of the larger discount brokerage firms follows.

List of Discount Brokers Which Have Self-Directed IRAs

Firm Name	*Headquarter Address*	*Telephone*	*Parent Company*	*IRA Fees*			*Allowable Investments*	*Minimum Commission*
				Set-up	*Annual*	*Termi-nation*		
Brown & Company	20 Winthrop Sq., Boston, MA 02110	800-225-6707	Chemical Bank	0	0	0	S,B,O	$21
Norstar Brokerage Corporation	67 Wall St., New York, NY 10055	800-221-4257	Norstar Bank	$25	$25	$50	S,B,O	30
Fidelity Bro-kerage	82 Devonshire St., Boston, MA 02109	800-544-6666	Fidelity Invest-ments	0	20*	10	MF**,S,B,O	30
Pacific Bro-kerage Service, Inc.	5757 Wilshire Blvd., Los Angeles, CA 90036	800-223-3242	None	25	25	50	S,B,O	25
T. Rowe Price Discount	100 E. Pratt St., Balti-more, MD 21202	800-638-5600	T. Rowe Investments	15	0	0	MF**,S,B,O	30
Quick & Reilly	120 Wall St., New York, NY 10005	800-672-7220	None	0	25	50	MF**,S,B,O	35

Firm Name	Headquarter Address	Telephone	Parent Company	IRA Fees			Allowable Investments	Minimum Commission
				Set-up	Annual	Termination		
Rose & Company	One Financial Plaza, Chicago, IL 60605	800-621-3700	Chase Manhattan Bank	0	0	0	S,B,O	35
Chas Schwab	101 Montgomery St., San Francisco, CA 94104	800-227-4444	Bank of America	0	0	0	MF,S,B,O	34
Muriel Siebert & Co.	444 Madison Ave., New York, NY 10022	800-USA-0711	None	30	35	2.50	S,B,O	34
StockCross	One Washington Mall, Boston, MA 02108	800-225-6196	None	25	25	50	S,B,O	25
Waterhouse Securities	44 Wall St., New York, NY 10005	800-327-7500	None	25	25	50	S,B,O	35

Index

PROBUS PUBLISHING COMPANY PRESENTS

Titles in Investment/Personal Finance

The Investor's Equation: Creating Wealth Through Undervalued Stocks, by William M. Bowen IV and Frank P. Ganucheau III. ISBN 0–917253–00–0.

Stock Index Options: Powerful New Tools for Investing, Hedging, and Speculating, by Donald T. Mesler. ISBN 0–917253–02–7.

Winning the Interest Rate Game: A Guide to Debt Options, by Frank J. Fabozzi. ISBN 0–917253–01–9.

Low Risk Strategies for the High Performance Investor, by Thomas C. Noddings. ISBN 0–917253–09–4.

Maximize Your Gains: Tax Strategies for Today's Investor, by Robert W. Richards. ISBN 0–917253–10–8.

Increasing Your Wealth in Good Times and Bad, by Eugene M. Lerner and Richard M. Koff. ISBN 0–917253–06–X.

The Insider's Edge: Maximizing Investment Profits Through Managed Futures Accounts, by Bertram Schuster and Howard Abell. ISBN 0– 917253–12–4.

Personal Economics: A Guide to Financial Health and Well-Being, by Robert A. Kennedy and Timothy J. Watts. ISBN 0–917253–08–6.

The New Mutual Fund Investment Advisor, by Richard C. Dorf. ISBN 0–917253–13–2.

Floating Rate Instruments: Characteristics, Valuation and Portfolio Strategies, by Frank J. Fabozzi. ISBN 0–917253–15–9.

Smarter Money: An Investment Game Plan for Those Who Made It and Want to Keep It, by Frank J. Fabozzi and Stephen Feldman. ISBN 0– 917253–16–7.

Warrants: Analysis and Investment Strategy, by Donald T. Mesler. ISBN 0–917253–25–6.

Mastering Your Money: The Complete Guide to Computerwise Personal Financial Management, by Colin K. Mick and Kerry Mason. ISBN 0– 917253–20–5.

Superhedging, by Thomas C. Noddings. ISBN 0–917253–21–3.

High Performance Futures Trading: Computerbased Strategies and Techniques, by William T. Taylor. ISBN 0–917253–22–1.

Executive Economics, by Timothy J. Watts. ISBN 0–917253–23–X.

Self-Directed IRAs for the Active Investor: Taking Charge of Building Your Nest Egg, by Peter D. Heerwagen. ISBN 0–917253–32–9.

The Investor's Desktop Portfolio Planner, by Geoffrey Hirt, Stanley Block, and Fred Jury. ISBN 0–917253–33–7.

The New Guide to Tax Sheltered Investments: How To Evaluate and Buy Tax-Favored Investments That Perform, by G. Timothy Haight and John C. Chanoski. ISBN 0–917253–30–2.

The Stock Index Futures Market: A Trader's Insights and Strategies, by B. Thomas Byrne, Jr. ISBN 0–917253–28–0.

The Trader's and Investor's Guide to Commodity Trading Systems, Software and Data Bases, by William T. Taylor. ISBN 0–917253–41–8.

Timing the Market: How to Profit in Bull and Bear Markets with Technical Analysis, by Weiss Research. ISBN 0–917253–37–X.

The Handbook of Mortgage-Backed Securities, by Frank J. Fabozzi. ISBN 0-917253-04-3.

Titles in Business

Revitalizing Your Business: Five Steps to Successfully Turning Around Your Company, by Edmund P. Freiermuth. ISBN 0–917253–05–1.

Compensating Yourself: Personal Income, Benefits and Tax Strategies for Business Owners, by Gerald I. Kalish. ISBN 0– 917253–07–8.

Using Consultants: A Consumer's Guide for Managers, by Thomas A. Easton and Ralph Conant. ISBN 0–917253–03–5.

Cutting Loose: Making the Transition From Employee to Entrepreneur, by Thomas A. Easton and Ralph W. Conant. ISBN 0– 917253–14–0.

What's What in American Business: Facts and Figures on the Biggest and the Best, by George Kurian. ISBN 0–917253–17–5.

Competing for Clients: The Complete Guide to Marketing and Promoting Professional Services, by Bruce Marcus. ISBN 0–917253– 26–4.

Compensating Your Sales Force: The Sales Executive's Book of Compensation Programs and Strategies, by W. G. Ryckman. ISBN 0–917253–38–8.

Leasing Industrial and Business Equipment: Strategies and Techniques for Lessors and Lessees, by Lloyd A. Haynes, Jr. ISBN 0–917253–31–0.

Not Heard on the Street: An Irreverent Dictionary of Wall Street, by Maurice Joy. ISBN 0–917253–40–x.

Public Relations for the Entrepreneur and the Growing Business: How to Use Public Relations to Increase Visibility and Create Opportunities For You and Your Company, by Norman R. Soderberg. ISBN 0–917253–35–3.

The Executive's Guide to Business and Economic Forecasting, by Charles E. Webster. ISBN 0–917253–36–1.

The Entrepreneur's Guide to Capital: More Than 40 Techniques for Capitalizing and Refinancing New and Growing Businesses, by Jennifer Lindsey. ISBN 0–917253–34–5.

The 101 Best Performing Companies in America, by Ronald N. Paul and James W. Taylor. ISBN 0–917253–39–6.

The Operating Executive's Handbook of Profit Planning Tools and Techniques, by Charles J. Woelfel and Charles D. Mecimore. ISBN 0–917253–24–8.

The Valuation of Privately-Held Businesses: State-of-the-Art Techniques for Buyers, Sellers and Their Advisors, by Irving L. Blackman. ISBN 0–917253–27–2.